bo
ow, a

Fine

MWENG
09013190

Cram101 Textbook Outlines to accompany:

Surface Water-Quality Modeling

Chapra, 1st Edition

An Academic Internet Publishers (AIPI) publication (c) 2007.

You have a discounted membership at www.Cram101.com with this book.

Get all of the practice tests for the chapters of this textbook, and access in-depth reference material for writing essays and papers. Here is an example from a Cram101 Biology text:

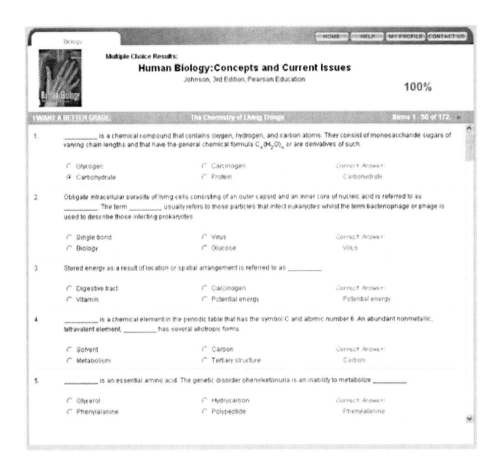

When you need problem solving help with math, stats, and other disciplines, www.Cram101.com will walk through the formulas and solutions step by step.

With Cram101.com online, you also have access to extensive reference material.

You will nail those essays and papers. Here is an example from a Cram101 Biology text:

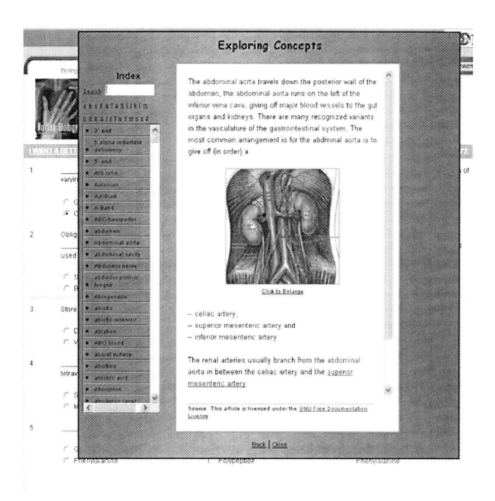

Visit **www.Cram101.com**, click Sign Up at the top of the screen, and enter DK73DW784 in the promo code box on the registration screen. Access to www.Cram101.com is normally $9.95, but because you have purchased this book, your access fee is only $4.95. Sign up and stop highlighting textbooks forever.

Learning System

Cram101 Textbook Outlines is a learning system. The notes in this book are the highlights of your textbook, you will never have to highlight a book again.

How to use this book. Take this book to class, it is your notebook for the lecture. The notes and highlights on the left hand side of the pages follow the outline and order of the textbook. All you have to do is follow along while your intructor presents the lecture. Circle the items emphasized in class and add other important information on the right side. With Cram101 Textbook Outlines you'll spend less time writing and more time listening. Learning becomes more efficient.

Cram101.com Online

Increase your studying efficiency by using Cram101.com's practice tests and online reference material. It is the perfect complement to Cram101 Textbook Outlines. Use self-teaching matching tests or simulate in-class testing with comprehensive multiple choice tests, or simply use Cram's true and false tests for quick review. Cram101.com even allows you to enter your in-class notes for an integrated studying format combining the textbook notes with your class notes.

Visit **www.Cram101.com**, click Sign Up at the top of the screen, and enter **DK73DW784** in the promo code box on the registration screen. Access to www.Cram101.com is normally $9.95, but because you have purchased this book, your access fee is only $4.95. Sign up and stop highlighting textbooks forever.

Surface Water-Quality Modeling
Chapra, 1st

CONTENTS

Surface Water-Quality Modeling
Chapra, 1st

CONTENTS (continued)

Pollution	Pollution is the introduction of substances or energy into the environment, resulting in deleterious effects of such a nature as to endanger human health, harm living resources and ecosystems, and impair or interfere with amenities and other legitimate uses of the environment.
Industrial Revolution	The Industrial Revolution was a major shift of technological, socioeconomic, and cultural conditions that occurred in the late 18th century and early 19th century in some Western countries. It began in Britain and spread throughout the world, a process that continues.
Potable water	Water of sufficient quality to serve as drinking water is termed potable water whether it is used as such or not.
Salinity	Salinity is the saltiness or dissolved salt content of a body of water. In oceanography, it has been traditional to express halinity not as percent, but as parts per thousand, which is approximately grams of salt per liter of solution.
Chlorophyll	Chlorophyll is a green pigment found in most plants, algae, and cyanobacteria.
Island	An island is any piece of land that is completely surrounded by water, above high tide. There are two main types of islands: continental islands and oceanic islands. There are also artificial islands. A grouping of geographically and/or geologically related islands is called an archipelago.
Atmosphere	An atmosphere is a layer of gases that may surround a material body of sufficient mass. The gases are attracted by the gravity of the body, and are retained for a longer duration if gravity is high and the atmosphere's temperature is low. Some planets consist mainly of various gases, and thus have very deep atmospheres.
Surface water	Water collecting on the ground or in a stream, river, lake, or wetland is called surface water; as opposed to groundwater. Surface water is naturally replenished by precipitation and naturally lost through discharge to the oceans, evaporation, and sub-surface seepage into the groundwater. Surface water is the largest source of fresh water.
Lake	A lake is a body of water or other liquid of considerable size contained on a body of land. A vast majority are fresh water, and lie in the Northern Hemisphere at higher latitudes. Most have a natural outflow in the form of a river or stream, but some do not, and lose water solely by evaporation and/or underground seepage.
Dredging	Dredging is an excavation activity or operation usually carried out at least partly underwater, in shallow seas or fresh water areas with the purpose of gathering up bottom sediments and disposing of them at a different location.
Phosphate	A phosphate, in inorganic chemistry, is a salt of phosphoric acid. In organic chemistry it is an ester of phosphoric acid.
Eutrophication	Eutrophication refers to an increase in the primary productivity of any ecosystem. Eutrophication is caused by the increase of chemical nutrients, typically compounds containing nitrogen or phosphorus. It may occur on land or in water.
Matter	Matter is the substance of which physical objects are composed. Matter can be solid, liquid, plasma or gas. It constitutes the observable universe.
Equilibrium	Equilibrium is the condition of a system in which competing influences are balanced.
Dynamic Equilibrium	A dynamic equilibrium occurs when two reversible processes occur at the same rate.
Bacteria	Bacteria are unicellular microorganisms. They are typically a few micrometres long and have many shapes including curved rods, spheres, rods, and spirals.
Benthos	Benthos are the organisms which live on, in, or near the seabed. Although the term derived from the Greek for "depths of the sea", the term is also used in freshwater biology to refer to organisms at the bottoms of freshwater bodies of water, such as lakes, rivers, and streams.

Go to **Cram101.com** for the Practice Tests for this Chapter.
And, **NEVER** highlight a book again!

Drainage	Drainage is the natural or artificial removal of surface and sub-surface water from a given area. Many agricultural soils need drainage to improve production or to manage water supplies.
Drainage basin	A drainage basin is a region of land where water from rain or snow melt drains downhill into a body of water, such as a river, lake, dam, estuary, wetland, sea or ocean. The drainage basin includes both the streams and rivers that convey the water as well as the land surfaces from which water drains into those channels. The drainage basin acts like a funnel - collecting all the water within the area covered by the basin and channeling it into a waterway.
Nonpoint sources	Nonpoint sources comes from many unidentifiable sources with no specific solution to rectify the proble, making it difficult to regulate. An example would be urban runnoff of items like oil, fertilizers, and lawn chemicals. As rainfall or snowmelt moves over and through the ground, it picks up and carries away natural and human-made pollutants.
Ecosystem	An ecosystem is a natural unit consisting of all plants, animals and micro organisms in an area functioning together with all the non living physical factors of the environment.
Phytoplankton	Phytoplankton are the autotrophic component of plankton. Most phytoplankton are too small to be individually seen with the unaided eye. However, when present in high enough numbers, they may appear as a green discoloration of the water due to the presence of chlorophyll within their cells.
Detritus	In biology, detritus is non-living particulate organic material. It typically includes the bodies of dead organisms or fragments of organisms or faecal material. Detritus is normally colonised by communities of microorganisms which act to decompose the material.
Carbon	Carbon is a chemical element. An abundant nonmetallic, tetravalent element, carbon has several allotropic forms. This element is the basis of the chemistry of all known life.
Carbon cycle	The carbon cycle is the biogeochemical cycle by which carbon is exchanged between the biosphere, geosphere, hydrosphere, and atmosphere of the Earth.
Food web	Food web refers to describe the feeding relationships between species in an ecological community. Typically a food web refers to a graph where only connections are recorded, and a food web or ecosystem network refers to a network where the connections are given weights representing the quantity of nutrients or energy being transferred.
Climate	Climate is the average and variations of weather over long periods of time. Climate zones can be defined using parameters such as temperature and rainfall.
Iceberg	An iceberg is a large piece of freshwater ice that has broken off from a snow-formed glacier or ice shelf and is floating in open water. Typically, only one ninth of the volume of an iceberg is above water. The shape of the remainder under the water can be difficult to surmise from looking at what is visible above the surface.
Diffusion	Diffusion is the net action of matter, particles or molecules, heat, momentum, or light whose end is to minimize a concentration gradient.
Sediment	Sediment is any particulate matter that can be transported by fluid flow and which eventually is deposited as a layer of solid particles on the bed or bottom of a body of water or other liquid.
Thermal	A thermal column is a column of rizing air in the lower altitudes of the Earth face=symbol>¢s atmosphere. Thermals are created by the uneven heating of the Earth face=symbol>¢s surface from solar radiation, and are an example of convection. The Sun warms the ground, which in turn warms the air directly above it.
Biochemical oxygen demand	Biochemical oxygen demand is a chemical procedure for determining how fast biological organisms use up oxygen in a body of water.
Stream	A stream is a body of water with a current, confined within a bed and banks. Streams are important as conduits in the water cycle, instruments in aquifer recharge, and corridors for fish and wildlife

Go to **Cram101.com** for the Practice Tests for this Chapter.

migration.

Thermocline

The thermocline is a layer within a body of water or air where the temperature changes rapidly with depth.

Storm

A storm is any disturbed state of an astronomical body's atmosphere, especially affecting its surface, and strongly implying severe weather. It may be marked by strong wind, thunder and lightning, heavy precipitation, such as ice, or wind transporting some substance through the atmosphere.

Porosity

Porosity is a measure of the void spaces in a material, and is measured as a fraction, between 0–1, or as a percentage between 0–100%.

Currents

Ocean currents are any more or less continuous, directed movement of ocean water that flows in one of the Earth's oceans.They are rivers of hot or cold water within the ocean. They are generated from the forces acting upon the water like the earth's rotation, the wind, the temperature and salinity differences and the gravitation of the moon.

Equilibrium	Equilibrium is the condition of a system in which competing influences are balanced.
Matter	Matter is the substance of which physical objects are composed. Matter can be solid, liquid, plasma or gas. It constitutes the observable universe.
Bacteria	Bacteria are unicellular microorganisms. They are typically a few micrometres long and have many shapes including curved rods, spheres, rods, and spirals.
Carbon	Carbon is a chemical element. An abundant nonmetallic, tetravalent element, carbon has several allotropic forms. This element is the basis of the chemistry of all known life.
Carbon dioxide	Carbon dioxide is a chemical compound, normally in a gaseous state, and is composed of one carbon and two oxygen atoms. It is often referred to by its formula CO_2. It is present in the Earth's atmosphere at a concentration of approximately .000383 by volume and is an important greenhouse gas due to its ability to absorb many infrared wavelengths of sunlight, and due to the length of time it stays in the atmosphere.
Photosynthesis	Photosynthesis generally, is the synthesis of triose phosphates from sunlight, carbon dioxide and water.
Ion	An ion is an atom or group of atoms which have lost or gained one or more electrons, making them negatively or positively charged.
Oxide	An oxide is a chemical compound containing an oxygen atom and other elements. Most of the earth's crust consists of them. They result when elements are oxidized by air.
Molecule	In chemistry, a molecule is defined as a sufficiently stable electrically neutral group of at least two atoms in a definite arrangement held together by strong chemical bonds.
Frequency	Frequency is the measurement of the number of occurrences of a repeated event per unit of time. It is also defined as the rate of change of phase of a sinusoidal waveform.
Phytoplankton	Phytoplankton are the autotrophic component of plankton. Most phytoplankton are too small to be individually seen with the unaided eye. However, when present in high enough numbers, they may appear as a green discoloration of the water due to the presence of chlorophyll within their cells.
Sediment	Sediment is any particulate matter that can be transported by fluid flow and which eventually is deposited as a layer of solid particles on the bed or bottom of a body of water or other liquid.
Lake	A lake is a body of water or other liquid of considerable size contained on a body of land. A vast majority are fresh water, and lie in the Northern Hemisphere at higher latitudes. Most have a natural outflow in the form of a river or stream, but some do not, and lose water solely by evaporation and/or underground seepage.
Population dynamics	Population dynamics is the study of marginal and long-term changes in the numbers, individual weights and age composition of individuals in one or several populations, and biological and environmental processes influencing those changes.
Fossil	Fossils are the mineralized or otherwise preserved remains or traces of animals, plants, and other organisms. The totality of fossils, both discovered and undiscovered, and their placement in fossiliferous rock formations and sedimentary layers is known as the fossil record.
Organic compound	An organic compound is any member of a large class of chemical compounds whose molecules contain carbon.
Organism	In biology and ecology, an organism is a living complex adaptive system of organs that influence each other in such a way that they function in some way as a stable whole.

Go to **Cram101.com** for the Practice Tests for this Chapter.

Phosphate

A phosphate, in inorganic chemistry, is a salt of phosphoric acid. In organic chemistry it is an ester of phosphoric acid.

Go to **Cram101.com** for the Practice Tests for this Chapter.

Lake	A lake is a body of water or other liquid of considerable size contained on a body of land. A vast majority are fresh water, and lie in the Northern Hemisphere at higher latitudes. Most have a natural outflow in the form of a river or stream, but some do not, and lose water solely by evaporation and/or underground seepage.
Matter	Matter is the substance of which physical objects are composed. Matter can be solid, liquid, plasma or gas. It constitutes the observable universe.
Atmosphere	An atmosphere is a layer of gases that may surround a material body of sufficient mass. The gases are attracted by the gravity of the body, and are retained for a longer duration if gravity is high and the atmosphere's temperature is low. Some planets consist mainly of various gases, and thus have very deep atmospheres.
Precipitation	Precipitation is any product of the condensation of atmospheric water vapor that is deposited on the earth's surface. It occurs when the atmosphere becomes saturated with water vapour and the water condenses and falls out of solution. Air becomes saturated via two processes, cooling and adding moisture.
Stream	A stream is a body of water with a current, confined within a bed and banks. Streams are important as conduits in the water cycle, instruments in aquifer recharge, and corridors for fish and wildlife migration.
Sediment	Sediment is any particulate matter that can be transported by fluid flow and which eventually is deposited as a layer of solid particles on the bed or bottom of a body of water or other liquid.
Equilibrium	Equilibrium is the condition of a system in which competing influences are balanced.
Dynamic Equilibrium	A dynamic equilibrium occurs when two reversible processes occur at the same rate.
Residence time	Residence time is a broadly useful concept that expresses how fast something moves through a system in equilibrium. It is the average time a substance spends within a specified region of space, such as a reservoir.
Molecule	In chemistry, a molecule is defined as a sufficiently stable electrically neutral group of at least two atoms in a definite arrangement held together by strong chemical bonds.
Evaporation	Evaporation is the process by which molecules in a liquid state become a gas.
Biochemical oxygen demand	Biochemical oxygen demand is a chemical procedure for determining how fast biological organisms use up oxygen in a body of water.
Dredging	Dredging is an excavation activity or operation usually carried out at least partly underwater, in shallow seas or fresh water areas with the purpose of gathering up bottom sediments and disposing of them at a different location.
Pesticide	The U.S Environmental Protection Agency defines a pesticide as "any substance or mixture of substances intended for preventing, destroying, repelling, or lessening the damage of any pest".

Delta	A delta is a landform where the mouth of a river flows into an ocean, sea, desert, estuary or lake. It builds up sediment outwards into the flat area which the river face=symbol>¢s flow encounters transported by the water and set down as the currents slow.
Amplitude	The amplitude is a nonnegative scalar measure of a wave's magnitude of oscillation, that is, the magnitude of the maximum disturbance in the medium during one wave cycle. When amplitude of sound wave changes, a listener would hear a change in pitch.
Frequency	Frequency is the measurement of the number of occurrences of a repeated event per unit of time. It is also defined as the rate of change of phase of a sinusoidal waveform.
Wave	A wave is a disturbance that propagates through space or spacetime, transferring energy and momentum and sometimes angular momentum.
Attenuation	Attenuation is the reduction in amplitude and intensity of a signal.
Lake	A lake is a body of water or other liquid of considerable size contained on a body of land. A vast majority are fresh water, and lie in the Northern Hemisphere at higher latitudes. Most have a natural outflow in the form of a river or stream, but some do not, and lose water solely by evaporation and/or underground seepage.
Residence time	Residence time is a broadly useful concept that expresses how fast something moves through a system in equilibrium. It is the average time a substance spends within a specified region of space, such as a reservoir.
Diurnal	A diurnal animal is an animal that is active during the daytime and rests during the night.
Photosynthesis	Photosynthesis generally, is the synthesis of triose phosphates from sunlight, carbon dioxide and water.
Stream	A stream is a body of water with a current, confined within a bed and banks. Streams are important as conduits in the water cycle, instruments in aquifer recharge, and corridors for fish and wildlife migration.
Pesticide	The U.S Environmental Protection Agency defines a pesticide as "any substance or mixture of substances intended for preventing, destroying, repelling, or lessening the damage of any pest".
Solar power	Solar power is Solar Radiation emitted from our sun. It has been used in many traditional technologies for centuries, and has come into widespread use where other power supplies are absent, such as in remote locations and in space.

Lake	A lake is a body of water or other liquid of considerable size contained on a body of land. A vast majority are fresh water, and lie in the Northern Hemisphere at higher latitudes. Most have a natural outflow in the form of a river or stream, but some do not, and lose water solely by evaporation and/or underground seepage.
Stream	A stream is a body of water with a current, confined within a bed and banks. Streams are important as conduits in the water cycle, instruments in aquifer recharge, and corridors for fish and wildlife migration.
Atmosphere	An atmosphere is a layer of gases that may surround a material body of sufficient mass. The gases are attracted by the gravity of the body, and are retained for a longer duration if gravity is high and the atmosphere's temperature is low. Some planets consist mainly of various gases, and thus have very deep atmospheres.
Radioactive decay	Radioactive decay is the process in which an unstable atomic nucleus loses energy by emitting radiation in the form of particles or electromagnetic waves.
Pesticide	The U.S Environmental Protection Agency defines a pesticide as "any substance or mixture of substances intended for preventing, destroying, repelling, or lessening the damage of any pest".

Lake	A lake is a body of water or other liquid of considerable size contained on a body of land. A vast majority are fresh water, and lie in the Northern Hemisphere at higher latitudes. Most have a natural outflow in the form of a river or stream, but some do not, and lose water solely by evaporation and/or underground seepage.
Sediment	Sediment is any particulate matter that can be transported by fluid flow and which eventually is deposited as a layer of solid particles on the bed or bottom of a body of water or other liquid.
Equilibrium	Equilibrium is the condition of a system in which competing influences are balanced.
Pesticide	The U.S Environmental Protection Agency defines a pesticide as "any substance or mixture of substances intended for preventing, destroying, repelling, or lessening the damage of any pest".
Matter	Matter is the substance of which physical objects are composed. Matter can be solid, liquid, plasma or gas. It constitutes the observable universe.
Atmosphere	An atmosphere is a layer of gases that may surround a material body of sufficient mass. The gases are attracted by the gravity of the body, and are retained for a longer duration if gravity is high and the atmosphere's temperature is low. Some planets consist mainly of various gases, and thus have very deep atmospheres.
Residence time	Residence time is a broadly useful concept that expresses how fast something moves through a system in equilibrium. It is the average time a substance spends within a specified region of space, such as a reservoir.
Global warming	Global warming is the increase in the average temperature of the Earth face=symbol>¢s near-surface air and oceans in recent decades and its projected continuation. An increase in global temperatures can in turn cause other changes, including sea level rise, and changes in the amount and pattern of precipitation resulting in floods and drought. There may also be changes in the frequency and intensity of extreme weather events.

Go to **Cram101.com** for the Practice Tests for this Chapter.
And, **NEVER** highlight a book again!

Lake	A lake is a body of water or other liquid of considerable size contained on a body of land. A vast majority are fresh water, and lie in the Northern Hemisphere at higher latitudes. Most have a natural outflow in the form of a river or stream, but some do not, and lose water solely by evaporation and/or underground seepage.
Pesticide	The U.S Environmental Protection Agency defines a pesticide as "any substance or mixture of substances intended for preventing, destroying, repelling, or lessening the damage of any pest".
Pollution	Pollution is the introduction of substances or energy into the environment, resulting in deleterious effects of such a nature as to endanger human health, harm living resources and ecosystems, and impair or interfere with amenities and other legitimate uses of the environment.

Diffusion	Diffusion is the net action of matter, particles or molecules, heat, momentum, or light whose end is to minimize a concentration gradient.
Lake	A lake is a body of water or other liquid of considerable size contained on a body of land. A vast majority are fresh water, and lie in the Northern Hemisphere at higher latitudes. Most have a natural outflow in the form of a river or stream, but some do not, and lose water solely by evaporation and/or underground seepage.
Matter	Matter is the substance of which physical objects are composed. Matter can be solid, liquid, plasma or gas. It constitutes the observable universe.
Gravitation	Gravitation, in everyday life, is most familiar as the agency that endows objects with weight. Gravitation is responsible for keeping the Earth and the other planets in their orbits around the Sun; for the formation of tides; and for various other phenomena that we observe. Gravitation is also the reason for the very existence of the Earth, the Sun, and most macroscopic objects in the universe; without it, matter would not have coalesced into these large masses, and life, as we know it, would not exist.
Tide	Tide refers to the cyclic rizing and falling of Earth's ocean surface caused by the tidal forces of the Moon and the sun acting on the oceans. They cause changes in the depth of the marine and estuarine water bodies and produce oscillating currents known as tidal streams, making prediction of tides important for coastal navigation.
Pollution	Pollution is the introduction of substances or energy into the environment, resulting in deleterious effects of such a nature as to endanger human health, harm living resources and ecosystems, and impair or interfere with amenities and other legitimate uses of the environment.
Tides	Tides are the cyclic rizing and falling of Earth's ocean surface caused by the tidal forces of the Moon and the sun acting on the oceans. Tides cause changes in the depth of the marine and estuarine water bodies and produce oscillating currents known as tidal streams, making prediction of tides important for coastal navigation.
Molecule	In chemistry, a molecule is defined as a sufficiently stable electrically neutral group of at least two atoms in a definite arrangement held together by strong chemical bonds.
Shoreline	A shoreline is the fringe of land at the edge of a large body of water, such as an ocean, sea, or lake. A strict definition is the strip of land along a water body that is alternately exposed and covered by waves and tides.
Convection	Convection in the most general terms refers to the movement of currents within fluids. Convection is one of the major modes of Heat and mass transfer. In fluids, convective heat and mass transfer take place through both diffusion and by advection, in which matter or heat is transported by the larger-scale motion of currents in the fluid.
Buoyancy	In physics, buoyancy is the upward force on an object produced by the surrounding fluid in which it is fully or partially immersed, due to the pressure difference of the fluid between the top and bottom of the object. The net upward buoyancy force is equal to the magnitude of the weight of fluid displaced by the body.
Thermal	A thermal column is a column of rizing air in the lower altitudes of the Earth face=symbol>¢s atmosphere. Thermals are created by the uneven heating of the Earth's surface from solar radiation, and are an example of convection. The Sun warms the ground, which in turn warms the air directly above it.
Residence time	Residence time is a broadly useful concept that expresses how fast something moves through a system in equilibrium. It is the average time a substance spends within a specified region of space, such as a reservoir.

Diffusion	Diffusion is the net action of matter, particles or molecules, heat, momentum, or light whose end is to minimize a concentration gradient.
Lake	A lake is a body of water or other liquid of considerable size contained on a body of land. A vast majority are fresh water, and lie in the Northern Hemisphere at higher latitudes. Most have a natural outflow in the form of a river or stream, but some do not, and lose water solely by evaporation and/or underground seepage.
Stream	A stream is a body of water with a current, confined within a bed and banks. Streams are important as conduits in the water cycle, instruments in aquifer recharge, and corridors for fish and wildlife migration.
Nonpoint sources	Nonpoint sources comes from many unidentifiable sources with no specific solution to rectify the proble, making it difficult to regulate. An example would be urban runnoff of items like oil, fertilizers, and lawn chemicals. As rainfall or snowmelt moves over and through the ground, it picks up and carries away natural and human-made pollutants.

Stream	A stream is a body of water with a current, confined within a bed and banks. Streams are important as conduits in the water cycle, instruments in aquifer recharge, and corridors for fish and wildlife migration.
Diffusion	Diffusion is the net action of matter, particles or molecules, heat, momentum, or light whose end is to minimize a concentration gradient.
Canals	Canals are artificial channels for water. There are two main types of canals: irrigation canals, which are used for the delivery of water, and waterways, which are transportation canals used for passage of goods and people, often connected to existing lakes, rivers, or oceans.
Groundwater	Groundwater is water located beneath the ground surface in soil pore spaces and in the fractures of geologic formations. Groundwater is recharged from, and eventually flows to, the surface naturally; natural discharge often occurs at springs and seeps, streams and can often form oases or wetlands.
Island	An island is any piece of land that is completely surrounded by water, above high tide. There are two main types of islands: continental islands and oceanic islands. There are also artificial islands. A grouping of geographically and/or geologically related islands is called an archipelago.
Herbicide	A herbicide is a pesticide used to kill unwanted plants. They kill specific targets while leaving the desired crop relatively unharmed.
Lake	A lake is a body of water or other liquid of considerable size contained on a body of land. A vast majority are fresh water, and lie in the Northern Hemisphere at higher latitudes. Most have a natural outflow in the form of a river or stream, but some do not, and lose water solely by evaporation and/or underground seepage.
Sediment	Sediment is any particulate matter that can be transported by fluid flow and which eventually is deposited as a layer of solid particles on the bed or bottom of a body of water or other liquid.

Go to **Cram101.com** for the Practice Tests for this Chapter.

| Lake | A lake is a body of water or other liquid of considerable size contained on a body of land. A vast majority are fresh water, and lie in the Northern Hemisphere at higher latitudes. Most have a natural outflow in the form of a river or stream, but some do not, and lose water solely by evaporation and/or underground seepage. |

Molecule	In chemistry, a molecule is defined as a sufficiently stable electrically neutral group of at least two atoms in a definite arrangement held together by strong chemical bonds.
Diffusion	Diffusion is the net action of matter, particles or molecules, heat, momentum, or light whose end is to minimize a concentration gradient.
Residence time	Residence time is a broadly useful concept that expresses how fast something moves through a system in equilibrium. It is the average time a substance spends within a specified region of space, such as a reservoir.
Thermodynamics	Thermodynamics is a branch of physics that studies the effects of changes in temperature, pressure, and volume on physical systems at the macroscopic scale by analyzing the collective motion of their particles using statistics.
Stream	A stream is a body of water with a current, confined within a bed and banks. Streams are important as conduits in the water cycle, instruments in aquifer recharge, and corridors for fish and wildlife migration.
Lake	A lake is a body of water or other liquid of considerable size contained on a body of land. A vast majority are fresh water, and lie in the Northern Hemisphere at higher latitudes. Most have a natural outflow in the form of a river or stream, but some do not, and lose water solely by evaporation and/or underground seepage.

Go to **Cram101.com** for the Practice Tests for this Chapter.

Node	A node is a point along a standing wave where the wave has minimal amplitude. This has implications in several fields. For instance, in a guitar string, the ends of the string are nodes. By changing the position of one of these nodes through frets, the guitarist changes the effective length of the vibrating string and thereby the note played.
Molecule	In chemistry, a molecule is defined as a sufficiently stable electrically neutral group of at least two atoms in a definite arrangement held together by strong chemical bonds.
Stream	A stream is a body of water with a current, confined within a bed and banks. Streams are important as conduits in the water cycle, instruments in aquifer recharge, and corridors for fish and wildlife migration.

Lake	A lake is a body of water or other liquid of considerable size contained on a body of land. A vast majority are fresh water, and lie in the Northern Hemisphere at higher latitudes. Most have a natural outflow in the form of a river or stream, but some do not, and lose water solely by evaporation and/or underground seepage.
Ion	An ion is an atom or group of atoms which have lost or gained one or more electrons, making them negatively or positively charged.
Stream	A stream is a body of water with a current, confined within a bed and banks. Streams are important as conduits in the water cycle, instruments in aquifer recharge, and corridors for fish and wildlife migration.
Pollution	Pollution is the introduction of substances or energy into the environment, resulting in deleterious effects of such a nature as to endanger human health, harm living resources and ecosystems, and impair or interfere with amenities and other legitimate uses of the environment.
Canals	Canals are artificial channels for water. There are two main types of canals: irrigation canals, which are used for the delivery of water, and waterways, which are transportation canals used for passage of goods and people, often connected to existing lakes, rivers, or oceans.
Hydrograph	A hydrograph plots the discharge of a river as a function of time. This activity can be in response to episodal event such as a flood.
Climate	Climate is the average and variations of weather over long periods of time. Climate zones can be defined using parameters such as temperature and rainfall.
Precipitation	Precipitation is any product of the condensation of atmospheric water vapor that is deposited on the earth's surface. It occurs when the atmosphere becomes saturated with water vapour and the water condenses and falls out of solution. Air becomes saturated via two processes, cooling and adding moisture.
Groundwater	Groundwater is water located beneath the ground surface in soil pore spaces and in the fractures of geologic formations. Groundwater is recharged from, and eventually flows to, the surface naturally; natural discharge often occurs at springs and seeps, streams and can often form oases or wetlands.
Storm	A storm is any disturbed state of an astronomical body's atmosphere, especially affecting its surface, and strongly implying severe weather. It may be marked by strong wind, thunder and lightning, heavy precipitation, such as ice, or wind transporting some substance through the atmosphere.
Channelization	Channelization secures a definite available depth for navigation; and the discharge of the river generally is amply sufficient for maintaining the impounded waterlevel, as well as providing the necessary water for locking.
Frequency	Frequency is the measurement of the number of occurrences of a repeated event per unit of time. It is also defined as the rate of change of phase of a sinusoidal waveform.
Gravitation	Gravitation, in everyday life, is most familiar as the agency that endows objects with weight. Gravitation is responsible for keeping the Earth and the other planets in their orbits around the Sun; for the formation of tides; and for various other phenomena that we observe. Gravitation is also the reason for the very existence of the Earth, the Sun, and most macroscopic objects in the universe; without it, matter would not have coalesced into these large masses, and life, as we know it, would not exist.
Gravel	Gravel is rock that is of a certain particle size range. In geology, gravel is any loose rock that is at least two millimeters in its largest dimension and no more than 75 millimeters.

35

Riprap	Riprap is rock or other material used to armor shorelines or stream banks against water erosion
Wave	A wave is a disturbance that propagates through space or spacetime, transferring energy and momentum and sometimes angular momentum.
Diffusion	Diffusion is the net action of matter, particles or molecules, heat, momentum, or light whose end is to minimize a concentration gradient.
Velocity	In physics, velocity is defined as the rate of change of displacement or the rate of displacement. Simply put, it is distance per units of time.
Hydrology	Hydrology is the study of the movement, distribution, and quality of water throughout the Earth, and thus addresses both the hydrologic cycle and water resources.

Ion	An ion is an atom or group of atoms which have lost or gained one or more electrons, making them negatively or positively charged.
Ecosystem	An ecosystem is a natural unit consisting of all plants, animals and micro organisms in an area functioning together with all the non living physical factors of the environment.
Salinity	Salinity is the saltiness or dissolved salt content of a body of water. In oceanography, it has been traditional to express halinity not as percent, but as parts per thousand, which is approximately grams of salt per liter of solution.
Tide	Tide refers to the cyclic rizing and falling of Earth's ocean surface caused by the tidal forces of the Moon and the sun acting on the oceans. They cause changes in the depth of the marine and estuarine water bodies and produce oscillating currents known as tidal streams, making prediction of tides important for coastal navigation.
Tides	Tides are the cyclic rizing and falling of Earth's ocean surface caused by the tidal forces of the Moon and the sun acting on the oceans. Tides cause changes in the depth of the marine and estuarine water bodies and produce oscillating currents known as tidal streams, making prediction of tides important for coastal navigation.
Surface runoff	Surface runoff is a term used to describe the flow of water, from rain, snowmelt, or other sources, over the land surface, and is a major component of the water cycle.
Groundwater	Groundwater is water located beneath the ground surface in soil pore spaces and in the fractures of geologic formations. Groundwater is recharged from, and eventually flows to, the surface naturally; natural discharge often occurs at springs and seeps, streams and can often form oases or wetlands.
Hydrology	Hydrology is the study of the movement, distribution, and quality of water throughout the Earth, and thus addresses both the hydrologic cycle and water resources.
Diffusion	Diffusion is the net action of matter, particles or molecules, heat, momentum, or light whose end is to minimize a concentration gradient.
Island	An island is any piece of land that is completely surrounded by water, above high tide. There are two main types of islands: continental islands and oceanic islands. There are also artificial islands. A grouping of geographically and/or geologically related islands is called an archipelago.
Stream	A stream is a body of water with a current, confined within a bed and banks. Streams are important as conduits in the water cycle, instruments in aquifer recharge, and corridors for fish and wildlife migration.
Lake	A lake is a body of water or other liquid of considerable size contained on a body of land. A vast majority are fresh water, and lie in the Northern Hemisphere at higher latitudes. Most have a natural outflow in the form of a river or stream, but some do not, and lose water solely by evaporation and/or underground seepage.
Matter	Matter is the substance of which physical objects are composed. Matter can be solid, liquid, plasma or gas. It constitutes the observable universe.
Sediment	Sediment is any particulate matter that can be transported by fluid flow and which eventually is deposited as a layer of solid particles on the bed or bottom of a body of water or other liquid.
Thermocline	The thermocline is a layer within a body of water or air where the temperature changes rapidly with depth.

Go to **Cram101.com** for the Practice Tests for this Chapter.

Go to **Cram101.com** for the Practice Tests for this Chapter.
And, **NEVER** highlight a book again!

Lake	A lake is a body of water or other liquid of considerable size contained on a body of land. A vast majority are fresh water, and lie in the Northern Hemisphere at higher latitudes. Most have a natural outflow in the form of a river or stream, but some do not, and lose water solely by evaporation and/or underground seepage.
Hydrology	Hydrology is the study of the movement, distribution, and quality of water throughout the Earth, and thus addresses both the hydrologic cycle and water resources.
Residence time	Residence time is a broadly useful concept that expresses how fast something moves through a system in equilibrium. It is the average time a substance spends within a specified region of space, such as a reservoir.
Thermal	A thermal column is a column of rizing air in the lower altitudes of the Earth face=symbol>¢s atmosphere. Thermals are created by the uneven heating of the Earth's surface from solar radiation, and are an example of convection. The Sun warms the ground, which in turn warms the air directly above it.
Bathymetry	Bathymetry is the study of underwater depth, of the third dimension of lake or ocean floors.
Groundwater	Groundwater is water located beneath the ground surface in soil pore spaces and in the fractures of geologic formations. Groundwater is recharged from, and eventually flows to, the surface naturally; natural discharge often occurs at springs and seeps, streams and can often form oases or wetlands.
Precipitation	Precipitation is any product of the condensation of atmospheric water vapor that is deposited on the earth's surface. It occurs when the atmosphere becomes saturated with water vapour and the water condenses and falls out of solution. Air becomes saturated via two processes, cooling and adding moisture.
Evaporation	Evaporation is the process by which molecules in a liquid state become a gas.
Weather	The weather is the set of all extant phenomena in a given atmosphere at a given time. The term usually refers to the activity of these phenomena over short periods, as opposed to the term climate, which refers to the average atmospheric conditions over longer periods of time.
Atmosphere	An atmosphere is a layer of gases that may surround a material body of sufficient mass. The gases are attracted by the gravity of the body, and are retained for a longer duration if gravity is high and the atmosphere's temperature is low. Some planets consist mainly of various gases, and thus have very deep atmospheres.
Bedrock	Bedrock is the native consolidated rock underlying the Earth's surface. Above the bedrock is usually an area of broken and weathered unconsolidated rock in the basal subsoil.
Latent heat	In thermochemistry, latent heat is the amount of energy in the form of heat released or absorbed by a substance during a change of phase - also called a phase transition. The term was introduced around 1750 by Joseph Black as derived from the Latin latere, to lie hidden. The term is now obsolete, replaced by "enthalpy of transformation".
Surface water	Water collecting on the ground or in a stream, river, lake, or wetland is called surface water; as opposed to groundwater. Surface water is naturally replenished by precipitation and naturally lost through discharge to the oceans, evaporation, and sub-surface seepage into the groundwater. Surface water is the largest source of fresh water.
Storm	A storm is any disturbed state of an astronomical body's atmosphere, especially affecting its surface, and strongly implying severe weather. It may be marked by strong wind, thunder and lightning, heavy precipitation, such as ice, or wind transporting some substance through the atmosphere.
Hydrograph	A hydrograph plots the discharge of a river as a function of time. This activity can be in

response to episodal event such as a flood.

Matter	Matter is the substance of which physical objects are composed. Matter can be solid, liquid, plasma or gas. It constitutes the observable universe.
Shoreline	A shoreline is the fringe of land at the edge of a large body of water, such as an ocean, sea, or lake. A strict definition is the strip of land along a water body that is alternately exposed and covered by waves and tides.
Diffusion	Diffusion is the net action of matter, particles or molecules, heat, momentum, or light whose end is to minimize a concentration gradient.
Currents	Ocean currents are any more or less continuous, directed movement of ocean water that flows in one of the Earth's oceans.They are rivers of hot or cold water within the ocean. They are generated from the forces acting upon the water like the earth's rotation, the wind, the temperature and salinity differences and the gravitation of the moon.
Bacteria	Bacteria are unicellular microorganisms. They are typically a few micrometres long and have many shapes including curved rods, spheres, rods, and spirals.

Go to **Cram101.com** for the Practice Tests for this Chapter.

Go to **Cram101.com** for the Practice Tests for this Chapter.
And, **NEVER** highlight a book again!

Aquatic	The term aquatic refers to water and can be either a noun or an adjective. Dictionary definitions do not specify what kind of water, although in both general use and in the sciences, the implication is often that of fresh water.
Matter	Matter is the substance of which physical objects are composed. Matter can be solid, liquid, plasma or gas. It constitutes the observable universe.
Eutrophication	Eutrophication refers to an increase in the primary productivity of any ecosystem. Eutrophication is caused by the increase of chemical nutrients, typically compounds containing nitrogen or phosphorus. It may occur on land or in water.
Sediment	Sediment is any particulate matter that can be transported by fluid flow and which eventually is deposited as a layer of solid particles on the bed or bottom of a body of water or other liquid.
Lake	A lake is a body of water or other liquid of considerable size contained on a body of land. A vast majority are fresh water, and lie in the Northern Hemisphere at higher latitudes. Most have a natural outflow in the form of a river or stream, but some do not, and lose water solely by evaporation and/or underground seepage.
Delta	A delta is a landform where the mouth of a river flows into an ocean, sea, desert, estuary or lake. It builds up sediment outwards into the flat area which the river face=symbol>¢s flow encounters transported by the water and set down as the currents slow.
Dam	A dam is a barrier across flowing water that obstructs, directs or slows down the flow, often creating a reservoir, lake or impoundment.
Stream	A stream is a body of water with a current, confined within a bed and banks. Streams are important as conduits in the water cycle, instruments in aquifer recharge, and corridors for fish and wildlife migration.
Drainage	Drainage is the natural or artificial removal of surface and sub-surface water from a given area. Many agricultural soils need drainage to improve production or to manage water supplies.
Drainage basin	A drainage basin is a region of land where water from rain or snow melt drains downhill into a body of water, such as a river, lake, dam, estuary, wetland, sea or ocean. The drainage basin includes both the streams and rivers that convey the water as well as the land surfaces from which water drains into those channels. The drainage basin acts like a funnel - collecting all the water within the area covered by the basin and channeling it into a waterway.
Photosynthesis	Photosynthesis generally, is the synthesis of triose phosphates from sunlight, carbon dioxide and water.
Erosion	Erosion is displacement of solids by the agents of ocean currents, wind, water, or ice by downward or down-slope movement in response to gravity or by living organisms.
Weathering	Weathering is the process of breaking down rocks, soils and their minerals through direct contact with the atmosphere. Weathering occurs without movement. Two main classifications of weathering processes exist. Mechanical or physical weathering involves the breakdown of rocks and soils through direct contact with atmospheric conditions. The second classification, chemical weathering, involves the direct effect of atmospheric chemicals in the breakdown of rocks, soils and minerals.
Bacteria	Bacteria are unicellular microorganisms. They are typically a few micrometres long and have many shapes including curved rods, spheres, rods, and spirals.
Phytoplankton	Phytoplankton are the autotrophic component of plankton. Most phytoplankton are too small to

be individually seen with the unaided eye. However, when present in high enough numbers, they may appear as a green discoloration of the water due to the presence of chlorophyll within their cells.

Precipitation

Precipitation is any product of the condensation of atmospheric water vapor that is deposited on the earth's surface. It occurs when the atmosphere becomes
saturated with water vapour and the water condenses and falls out of solution. Air becomes saturated via two processes, cooling and adding moisture.

Particulates

Particulates are tiny particles of solid or liquid suspended in a gas. They range in size from less than 10 nanometres to more than 100 micrometres in diameter.

Electron

The electron is a fundamental subatomic particle that carries a negative electric charge.

Carbon

Carbon is a chemical element. An abundant nonmetallic, tetravalent element, carbon has several allotropic forms. This element is the basis of the chemistry of all known life.

Carbon dioxide

Carbon dioxide is a chemical compound, normally in a gaseous state, and is composed of one carbon and two oxygen atoms. It is often referred to by its formula CO_2. It is present in the Earth's atmosphere at a concentration of approximately .000383 by
volume and is an important greenhouse gas due to its ability to absorb many infrared wavelengths of sunlight, and due to the length of time it stays in the atmosphere.

Gravitation

Gravitation, in everyday life, is most familiar as the agency that endows objects with weight. Gravitation is responsible for keeping the Earth and the other planets in their orbits around the Sun; for the formation of tides; and for various other phenomena that we observe. Gravitation is also the reason for the very existence of the Earth, the Sun, and most macroscopic objects in the universe; without it, matter would not have coalesced into these large masses, and life, as we know it, would not exist.

Viscosity

Viscosity is a measure of the resistance of a fluid to deform under shear stress. It is commonly perceived as "thickness", or resistance to flow. Viscosity describes a fluid face=symbol>¢s internal resistance to flow and may be thought of as a measure of fluid friction.

Clay

Clay is a term used to describe a group of hydrous aluminium phyllosilicate minerals, that are typically less than 2 micrometres in diameter. Clay consists of a variety of phyllosilicate minerals rich in silicon and aluminium oxides and hydroxides which include variable amounts of structural water. Clays are generally formed by the chemical weathering of silicate-bearing rocks by carbonic acid but some are formed by hydrothermal activity.

Upwelling

Upwelling is an oceanographic phenomenon that involves wind-driven motion of dense, cooler, and usually nutrient-rich water towards the ocean surface, replacing the warmer, usually nutrient-deplete surface water.

Porosity

Porosity is a measure of the void spaces in a material, and is measured as a fraction, between 0–1, or as a percentage between 0–100%.

Diffusion

Diffusion is the net action of matter, particles or molecules, heat, momentum, or light whose end is to minimize a concentration gradient.

Compaction

Compaction is the process of a material being more closely packed together.

Radioactive decay

Radioactive decay is the process in which an unstable atomic nucleus loses energy by emitting radiation in the form of particles or electromagnetic waves.

Terrestrial

Terrestrial refers to things having to do with the land or with the planet Earth.

Fossil

Fossils are the mineralized or otherwise preserved remains or traces of animals, plants, and other organisms. The totality of fossils, both discovered and undiscovered, and their

placement in fossiliferous rock formations and sedimentary layers is known as the fossil record.

Fetch

Fetch is a term for the length of water over which a given wind has blown. It is used in geography and meteorology and is usually associated with coastal erosion. It plays a large part in longshore drift as well.

Wave

A wave is a disturbance that propagates through space or spacetime, transferring energy and momentum and sometimes angular momentum.

Wavelength

In physics, wavelength is the distance between repeating units of a propagating wave of a given frequency. It is commonly designated by the Greek letter lambda. Examples of wave-like phenonomena are light, water waves, and sound waves. Wavelength of a sine wave.In a wave, a property varies with the position.

Storm

A storm is any disturbed state of an astronomical body's atmosphere, especially affecting its surface, and strongly implying severe weather. It may be marked by strong wind, thunder and lightning, heavy precipitation, such as ice, or wind transporting some substance through the atmosphere.

Residence time

Residence time is a broadly useful concept that expresses how fast something moves through a system in equilibrium. It is the average time a substance spends within a specified region of space, such as a reservoir.

Drainage	Drainage is the natural or artificial removal of surface and sub-surface water from a given area. Many agricultural soils need drainage to improve production or to manage water supplies.
Drainage basin	A drainage basin is a region of land where water from rain or snow melt drains downhill into a body of water, such as a river, lake, dam, estuary, wetland, sea or ocean. The drainage basin includes both the streams and rivers that convey the water as well as the land surfaces from which water drains into those channels. The drainage basin acts like a funnel - collecting all the water within the area covered by the basin and channeling it into a waterway.
Currents	Ocean currents are any more or less continuous, directed movement of ocean water that flows in one of the Earth's oceans.They are rivers of hot or cold water within the ocean. They are generated from the forces acting upon the water like the earth's rotation, the wind, the temperature and salinity differences and the gravitation of the moon.
Pollution	Pollution is the introduction of substances or energy into the environment, resulting in deleterious effects of such a nature as to endanger human health, harm living resources and ecosystems, and impair or interfere with amenities and other legitimate uses of the environment.
Ecology	Ecology is the scientific study of the distribution and abundance of living organisms and how the distribution and abundance are affected by interactions between the organisms and their environment.
Stream	A stream is a body of water with a current, confined within a bed and banks. Streams are important as conduits in the water cycle, instruments in aquifer recharge, and corridors for fish and wildlife migration.
Dredging	Dredging is an excavation activity or operation usually carried out at least partly underwater, in shallow seas or fresh water areas with the purpose of gathering up bottom sediments and disposing of them at a different location.
Algae	Algae encompass several groups of relatively simple living aquatic organisms that capture light energy through photosynthesis, using it to convert inorganic substances into organic matter.
Shoreline	A shoreline is the fringe of land at the edge of a large body of water, such as an ocean, sea, or lake. A strict definition is the strip of land along a water body that is alternately exposed and covered by waves and tides.
Lake	A lake is a body of water or other liquid of considerable size contained on a body of land. A vast majority are fresh water, and lie in the Northern Hemisphere at higher latitudes. Most have a natural outflow in the form of a river or stream, but some do not, and lose water solely by evaporation and/or underground seepage.
Aquatic	The term aquatic refers to water and can be either a noun or an adjective. Dictionary definitions do not specify what kind of water, although in both general use and in the sciences, the implication is often that of fresh water.
Photosynthesis	Photosynthesis generally, is the synthesis of triose phosphates from sunlight, carbon dioxide and water.
Organism	In biology and ecology, an organism is a living complex adaptive system of organs that influence each other in such a way that they function in some way as a stable whole.
Biomass	Biomass, in the energy production industry, refers to living and recently dead biological material which can be used as fuel or for industrial production. Most commonly, biomass

Go to **Cram101.com** for the Practice Tests for this Chapter.

refers to plant matter grown for use as biofuel, but it also includes plant or animal matter used for production of fibres, chemicals or heat. Biomass may also include biodegradable wastes that can be burnt as fuel. It excludes organic material which has been transformed by geological processes into substances such as coal or petroleum.

Frequency	Frequency is the measurement of the number of occurrences of a repeated event per unit of time. It is also defined as the rate of change of phase of a sinusoidal waveform.
Island	An island is any piece of land that is completely surrounded by water, above high tide. There are two main types of islands: continental islands and oceanic islands. There are also artificial islands. A grouping of geographically and/or geologically related islands is called an archipelago.
Matter	Matter is the substance of which physical objects are composed. Matter can be solid, liquid, plasma or gas. It constitutes the observable universe.
Chlorophyll	Chlorophyll is a green pigment found in most plants, algae, and cyanobacteria.
Bacteria	Bacteria are unicellular microorganisms. They are typically a few micrometres long and have many shapes including curved rods, spheres, rods, and spirals.
Thermal	A thermal column is a column of rizing air in the lower altitudes of the Earth face=symbol>¢s atmosphere. Thermals are created by the uneven heating of the Earth's surface from solar radiation, and are an example of convection. The Sun warms the ground, which in turn warms the air directly above it.
Phytoplankton	Phytoplankton are the autotrophic component of plankton. Most phytoplankton are too small to be individually seen with the unaided eye. However, when present in high enough numbers, they may appear as a green discoloration of the water due to the presence of chlorophyll within their cells.
Diffusion	Diffusion is the net action of matter, particles or molecules, heat, momentum, or light whose end is to minimize a concentration gradient.

52

Go to **Cram101.com** for the Practice Tests for this Chapter.

Pollution	Pollution is the introduction of substances or energy into the environment, resulting in deleterious effects of such a nature as to endanger human health, harm living resources and ecosystems, and impair or interfere with amenities and other legitimate uses of the environment.
Biochemical oxygen demand	Biochemical oxygen demand is a chemical procedure for determining how fast biological organisms use up oxygen in a body of water.
Photosynthesis	Photosynthesis generally, is the synthesis of triose phosphates from sunlight, carbon dioxide and water.
Sediment	Sediment is any particulate matter that can be transported by fluid flow and which eventually is deposited as a layer of solid particles on the bed or bottom of a body of water or other liquid.
Pathogen	A pathogen is a biological agent that causes disease or illness to its host.
Bacteria	Bacteria are unicellular microorganisms. They are typically a few micrometres long and have many shapes including curved rods, spheres, rods, and spirals.
Solar power	Solar power is Solar Radiation emitted from our sun. It has been used in many traditional technologies for centuries, and has come into widespread use where other power supplies are absent, such as in remote locations and in space.
Carbon	Carbon is a chemical element. An abundant nonmetallic, tetravalent element, carbon has several allotropic forms. This element is the basis of the chemistry of all known life.
Carbon dioxide	Carbon dioxide is a chemical compound, normally in a gaseous state, and is composed of one carbon and two oxygen atoms. It is often referred to by its formula CO_2. It is present in the Earth's atmosphere at a concentration of approximately .000383 by volume and is an important greenhouse gas due to its ability to absorb many infrared wavelengths of sunlight, and due to the length of time it stays in the atmosphere.
Matter	Matter is the substance of which physical objects are composed. Matter can be solid, liquid, plasma or gas. It constitutes the observable universe.
Stream	A stream is a body of water with a current, confined within a bed and banks. Streams are important as conduits in the water cycle, instruments in aquifer recharge, and corridors for fish and wildlife migration.
Algae	Algae encompass several groups of relatively simple living aquatic organisms that capture light energy through photosynthesis, using it to convert inorganic substances into organic matter.
Aquatic	The term aquatic refers to water and can be either a noun or an adjective. Dictionary definitions do not specify what kind of water, although in both general use and in the sciences, the implication is often that of fresh water.
Island	An island is any piece of land that is completely surrounded by water, above high tide. There are two main types of islands: continental islands and oceanic islands. There are also artificial islands. A grouping of geographically and/or geologically related islands is called an archipelago.
Oxide	An oxide is a chemical compound containing an oxygen atom and other elements. Most of the earth's crust consists of them. They result when elements are oxidized by air.
Atmosphere	An atmosphere is a layer of gases that may surround a material body of sufficient mass. The gases are attracted by the gravity of the body, and are retained for a longer duration if gravity is high and the atmosphere's temperature is low. Some

Go to **Cram101.com** for the Practice Tests for this Chapter.

planets consist mainly of various gases, and thus have very deep atmospheres.

Equilibrium Equilibrium is the condition of a system in which competing influences are balanced.

Closed system In thermodynamics, a closed system can exchange heat and work, but not matter, with its surroundings.

Sulfur Sulfur or sulphur is the chemical element that has the symbol S and atomic number 16. It is an abundant, tasteless, multivalent non-metal. Sulfur, in its native form, is a yellow crystalline solid. In nature, it can be found as the pure element or as sulfide and sulfate minerals. It is an essential element for life and is found in two amino acids, cysteine and methionine.

Sulfur dioxide Sulfur dioxide is a chemical compound with the formula SO_2. This important gas is the main product from the combustion of sulfur compounds and is of significant environmental concern. Sulphur dioxide is produced by volcanoes and in various industrial processes.

Salinity Salinity is the saltiness or dissolved salt content of a body of water. In oceanography, it has been traditional to express halinity not as percent, but as parts per thousand, which is approximately grams of salt per liter of solution.

Water vapor Water vapor is the gas phase of water. Water vapor is one state of the water cycle within the hydrosphere. Water vapor can be produced from the evaporation of liquid water or from the sublimation of ice. Under normal atmospheric conditions, water vapor is continuously evaporating and condensing.

Vapor Vapor is the gas phase component of a another state of matter which does not completely fill its container. It is distinguished from the pure gas phase by the presence of the same substance in another state of matter. Hence when a liquid has completely evaporated, it is said that the system has been completely transformed to the gas phase.

Lake A lake is a body of water or other liquid of considerable size contained on a body of land. A vast majority are fresh water, and lie in the Northern Hemisphere at higher latitudes. Most have a natural outflow in the form of a river or stream, but some do not, and lose water solely by evaporation and/or underground seepage.

Diffusion Diffusion is the net action of matter, particles or molecules, heat, momentum, or light whose end is to minimize a concentration gradient.

Island	An island is any piece of land that is completely surrounded by water, above high tide. There are two main types of islands: continental islands and oceanic islands. There are also artificial islands. A grouping of geographically and/or geologically related islands is called an archipelago.
Diffusion	Diffusion is the net action of matter, particles or molecules, heat, momentum, or light whose end is to minimize a concentration gradient.
Equilibrium	Equilibrium is the condition of a system in which competing influences are balanced.
Atmosphere	An atmosphere is a layer of gases that may surround a material body of sufficient mass. The gases are attracted by the gravity of the body, and are retained for a longer duration if gravity is high and the atmosphere's temperature is low. Some planets consist mainly of various gases, and thus have very deep atmospheres.
Stream	A stream is a body of water with a current, confined within a bed and banks. Streams are important as conduits in the water cycle, instruments in aquifer recharge, and corridors for fish and wildlife migration.
Valley	In geology, a valley is a depression with predominant extent in one direction. The terms U-shaped and V-shaped are descriptive terms of geography to characterize the form of valleys. Most valleys belong to one of these two main types or a mixture of them, at least with respect of the cross section of the slopes or hillsides.
Dam	A dam is a barrier across flowing water that obstructs, directs or slows down the flow, often creating a reservoir, lake or impoundment.
Lake	A lake is a body of water or other liquid of considerable size contained on a body of land. A vast majority are fresh water, and lie in the Northern Hemisphere at higher latitudes. Most have a natural outflow in the form of a river or stream, but some do not, and lose water solely by evaporation and/or underground seepage.
Matter	Matter is the substance of which physical objects are composed. Matter can be solid, liquid, plasma or gas. It constitutes the observable universe.
Sediment	Sediment is any particulate matter that can be transported by fluid flow and which eventually is deposited as a layer of solid particles on the bed or bottom of a body of water or other liquid.
Currents	Ocean currents are any more or less continuous, directed movement of ocean water that flows in one of the Earth's oceans.They are rivers of hot or cold water within the ocean. They are generated from the forces acting upon the water like the earth's rotation, the wind, the temperature and salinity differences and the gravitation of the moon.
Carbon	Carbon is a chemical element. An abundant nonmetallic, tetravalent element, carbon has several allotropic forms. This element is the basis of the chemistry of all known life.
Carbon dioxide	Carbon dioxide is a chemical compound, normally in a gaseous state, and is composed of one carbon and two oxygen atoms. It is often referred to by its formula $CO2$. It is present in the Earth's atmosphere at a concentration of approximately .000383 by volume and is an important greenhouse gas due to its ability to absorb many infrared wavelengths of sunlight, and due to the length of time it stays in the atmosphere.
Toxicity	Toxicity is a measure of the degree to which something is toxic or poisonous. Toxicity can refer to the effect on a whole organism, such as a human or a bacterium or a plant, or to a substructure, such as a cell or an organ.
Water vapor	Water vapor is the gas phase of water. Water vapor is one state of the water cycle within the hydrosphere. Water vapor can be produced from the evaporation of liquid water or from the

Go to **Cram101.com** for the Practice Tests for this Chapter.

	sublimation of ice. Under normal atmospheric conditions, water vapor is continuously evaporating and condensing.
Vapor	Vapor is the gas phase component of a another state of matter which does not completely fill its container. It is distinguished from the pure gas phase by the presence of the same substance in another state of matter. Hence when a liquid has completely evaporated, it is said that the system has been completely transformed to the gas phase.
Diurnal	A diurnal animal is an animal that is active during the daytime and rests during the night.
Photosynthesis	Photosynthesis generally, is the synthesis of triose phosphates from sunlight, carbon dioxide and water.
Hydrocarbon	In organic chemistry, a hydrocarbon is an organic compound consisting entirely of hydrogen and carbon. With relation to chemical terminology, aromatic hydrocarbons or arenes, alkanes, alkenes and alkyne-based compounds composed entirely of carbon or hydrogen are referred to as "Pure" hydrocarbons, whereas other hydrocarbons with bonded compounds or impurities of sulphur or nitrogen, are referred to as "impure", and remain somewhat erroneously referred to as hydrocarbons.
Residence time	Residence time is a broadly useful concept that expresses how fast something moves through a system in equilibrium. It is the average time a substance spends within a specified region of space, such as a reservoir.
Altitude	Altitude is the elevation of an object from a known level or datum. Common datums are mean sea level and the surface of the World Geodetic System geoid, used by Global Positioning System. In aviation, altitude is measured in feet. For non-aviation uses, altitude may be measured in other units such as metres or miles.

Ion	An ion is an atom or group of atoms which have lost or gained one or more electrons, making them negatively or positively charged.
Stream	A stream is a body of water with a current, confined within a bed and banks. Streams are important as conduits in the water cycle, instruments in aquifer recharge, and corridors for fish and wildlife migration.
Matter	Matter is the substance of which physical objects are composed. Matter can be solid, liquid, plasma or gas. It constitutes the observable universe.
Nonpoint sources	Nonpoint sources comes from many unidentifiable sources with no specific solution to rectify the proble, making it difficult to regulate. An example would be urban runoff of items like oil, fertilizers, and lawn chemicals. As rainfall or snowmelt moves over and through the ground, it picks up and carries away natural and human-made pollutants.
Atmosphere	An atmosphere is a layer of gases that may surround a material body of sufficient mass. The gases are attracted by the gravity of the body, and are retained for a longer duration if gravity is high and the atmosphere's temperature is low. Some planets consist mainly of various gases, and thus have very deep atmospheres.
Hydrology	Hydrology is the study of the movement, distribution, and quality of water throughout the Earth, and thus addresses both the hydrologic cycle and water resources.
Salinity	Salinity is the saltiness or dissolved salt content of a body of water. In oceanography, it has been traditional to express halinity not as percent, but as parts per thousand, which is approximately grams of salt per liter of solution.
Altitude	Altitude is the elevation of an object from a known level or datum. Common datums are mean sea level and the surface of the World Geodetic System geoid, used by Global Positioning System. In aviation, altitude is measured in feet. For non-aviation uses, altitude may be measured in other units such as metres or miles.
Lake	A lake is a body of water or other liquid of considerable size contained on a body of land. A vast majority are fresh water, and lie in the Northern Hemisphere at higher latitudes. Most have a natural outflow in the form of a river or stream, but some do not, and lose water solely by evaporation and/or underground seepage.
Residence time	Residence time is a broadly useful concept that expresses how fast something moves through a system in equilibrium. It is the average time a substance spends within a specified region of space, such as a reservoir.

Go to **Cram101.com** for the Practice Tests for this Chapter.

Hydrology	Hydrology is the study of the movement, distribution, and quality of water throughout the Earth, and thus addresses both the hydrologic cycle and water resources.
Stream	A stream is a body of water with a current, confined within a bed and banks. Streams are important as conduits in the water cycle, instruments in aquifer recharge, and corridors for fish and wildlife migration.
Erosion	Erosion is displacement of solids by the agents of ocean currents, wind, water, or ice by downward or down-slope movement in response to gravity or by living organisms.
Leaching	Leaching is the process of extracting a substance from a solid by dissolving it in a liquid.
Sediment	Sediment is any particulate matter that can be transported by fluid flow and which eventually is deposited as a layer of solid particles on the bed or bottom of a body of water or other liquid.
Phytoplankton	Phytoplankton are the autotrophic component of plankton. Most phytoplankton are too small to be individually seen with the unaided eye. However, when present in high enough numbers, they may appear as a green discoloration of the water due to the presence of chlorophyll within their cells.
Matter	Matter is the substance of which physical objects are composed. Matter can be solid, liquid, plasma or gas. It constitutes the observable universe.
Diffusion	Diffusion is the net action of matter, particles or molecules, heat, momentum, or light whose end is to minimize a concentration gradient.
Photosynthesis	Photosynthesis generally, is the synthesis of triose phosphates from sunlight, carbon dioxide and water.
Nonpoint sources	Nonpoint sources comes from many unidentifiable sources with no specific solution to rectify the proble, making it difficult to regulate. An example would be urban runoff of items like oil, fertilizers, and lawn chemicals. As rainfall or snowmelt moves over and through the ground, it picks up and carries away natural and human-made pollutants.
Pollution	Pollution is the introduction of substances or energy into the environment, resulting in deleterious effects of such a nature as to endanger human health, harm living resources and ecosystems, and impair or interfere with amenities and other legitimate uses of the environment.
Benthos	Benthos are the organisms which live on, in, or near the seabed. Although the term derived from the Greek for "depths of the sea", the term is also used in freshwater biology to refer to organisms at the bottoms of freshwater bodies of water, such as lakes, rivers, and streams.
Leachate	Leachate is the liquid produced when water percolates through any permeable material. It can contain either dissolved or suspended material, or usually both. This liquid is most commonly found in association with landfills, where rain percolates through the waste and reacts with the products of decomposition, chemicals and other materials in the waste to produce the leachate.

Go to **Cram101.com** for the Practice Tests for this Chapter.

Nitrogen	Nitrogen is a chemical element which has the symbol N and atomic number 7. Elemental nitrogen is a colorless, odourless, tasteless and mostly inert diatomic gas at standard conditions, constituting 78.1% by volume of Earth's atmosphere.
Nitrogen cycle	The nitrogen cycle is the biogeochemical cycle that describes the transformations of nitrogen and nitrogen-containing compounds in nature.
Eutrophication	Eutrophication refers to an increase in the primary productivity of any ecosystem. Eutrophication is caused by the increase of chemical nutrients, typically compounds containing nitrogen or phosphorus. It may occur on land or in water.
Pollution	Pollution is the introduction of substances or energy into the environment, resulting in deleterious effects of such a nature as to endanger human health, harm living resources and ecosystems, and impair or interfere with amenities and other legitimate uses of the environment.
Toxicity	Toxicity is a measure of the degree to which something is toxic or poisonous. Toxicity can refer to the effect on a whole organism, such as a human or a bacterium or a plant, or to a substructure, such as a cell or an organ.
Denitrification	Denitrification is the process of reducing nitrate and nitrite, highly oxidised forms of nitrogen available for consumption by many groups of organisms, into gaseous nitrogen, which is far less accessible to life forms but makes up the bulk of our atmosphere. The process is performed by heterotrophic bacteria from all main proteolytic groups.
Atmosphere	An atmosphere is a layer of gases that may surround a material body of sufficient mass. The gases are attracted by the gravity of the body, and are retained for a longer duration if gravity is high and the atmosphere's temperature is low. Some planets consist mainly of various gases, and thus have very deep atmospheres.
Algae	Algae encompass several groups of relatively simple living aquatic organisms that capture light energy through photosynthesis, using it to convert inorganic substances into organic matter.
Bacteria	Bacteria are unicellular microorganisms. They are typically a few micrometres long and have many shapes including curved rods, spheres, rods, and spirals.
Nonpoint sources	Nonpoint sources comes from many unidentifiable sources with no specific solution to rectify the proble, making it difficult to regulate. An example would be urban runoff of items like oil, fertilizers, and lawn chemicals. As rainfall or snowmelt moves over and through the ground, it picks up and carries away natural and human-made pollutants.
Ion	An ion is an atom or group of atoms which have lost or gained one or more electrons, making them negatively or positively charged.
Equilibrium	Equilibrium is the condition of a system in which competing influences are balanced.
Stream	A stream is a body of water with a current, confined within a bed and banks. Streams are important as conduits in the water cycle, instruments in aquifer recharge, and corridors for fish and wildlife migration.
Photosynthesis	Photosynthesis generally, is the synthesis of triose phosphates from sunlight, carbon dioxide and water.
Carbon	Carbon is a chemical element. An abundant nonmetallic, tetravalent element, carbon has several allotropic forms. This element is the basis of the chemistry of all known life.
Carbon dioxide	Carbon dioxide is a chemical compound, normally in a gaseous state, and is composed of one carbon and two oxygen atoms. It is often referred to by its formula $CO2$. It is present in the Earth's atmosphere at a concentration of approximately .000383 by

Go to **Cram101.com** for the Practice Tests for this Chapter.

volume and is an important greenhouse gas due to its ability to absorb many infrared wavelengths of sunlight, and due to the length of time it stays in the atmosphere.

Aquatic	The term aquatic refers to water and can be either a noun or an adjective. Dictionary definitions do not specify what kind of water, although in both general use and in the sciences, the implication is often that of fresh water.
Oxide	An oxide is a chemical compound containing an oxygen atom and other elements. Most of the earth's crust consists of them. They result when elements are oxidized by air.
Matter	Matter is the substance of which physical objects are composed. Matter can be solid, liquid, plasma or gas. It constitutes the observable universe.
Diurnal	A diurnal animal is an animal that is active during the daytime and rests during the night.
Phosphate	A phosphate, in inorganic chemistry, is a salt of phosphoric acid. In organic chemistry it is an ester of phosphoric acid.
Aerobic	An aerobic organism is an organism that has an oxygen based metabolism
Sediment	Sediment is any particulate matter that can be transported by fluid flow and which eventually is deposited as a layer of solid particles on the bed or bottom of a body of water or other liquid.
Residence time	Residence time is a broadly useful concept that expresses how fast something moves through a system in equilibrium. It is the average time a substance spends within a specified region of space, such as a reservoir.

Go to **Cram101.com** for the Practice Tests for this Chapter.

Go to **Cram101.com** for the Practice Tests for this Chapter.
And, **NEVER** highlight a book again!

Delta	A delta is a landform where the mouth of a river flows into an ocean, sea, desert, estuary or lake. It builds up sediment outwards into the flat area which the river face=symbol>¢s flow encounters transported by the water and set down as the currents slow.
Photosynthesis	Photosynthesis generally, is the synthesis of triose phosphates from sunlight, carbon dioxide and water.
Nonpoint sources	Nonpoint sources comes from many unidentifiable sources with no specific solution to rectify the proble, making it difficult to regulate. An example would be urban runnoff of items like oil, fertilizers, and lawn chemicals. As rainfall or snowmelt moves over and through the ground, it picks up and carries away natural and human-made pollutants.
Stream	A stream is a body of water with a current, confined within a bed and banks. Streams are important as conduits in the water cycle, instruments in aquifer recharge, and corridors for fish and wildlife migration.
Bacteria	Bacteria are unicellular microorganisms. They are typically a few micrometres long and have many shapes including curved rods, spheres, rods, and spirals.
Matter	Matter is the substance of which physical objects are composed. Matter can be solid, liquid, plasma or gas. It constitutes the observable universe.
Extinction	In biology and ecology, extinction is the cessation of existence of a species or group of taxa, reducing biodiversity. The moment of extinction is generally considered to be the death of the last individual of that species.
Turbidity	Turbidity is a cloudiness or haziness of water caused by individual particles that are generally invisible to the naked eye, thus being much like smoke in air. Turbidity is generally caused by phytoplankton. Measurement of turbidity is a key test of water quality.
Diurnal	A diurnal animal is an animal that is active during the daytime and rests during the night.
Phytoplankton	Phytoplankton are the autotrophic component of plankton. Most phytoplankton are too small to be individually seen with the unaided eye. However, when present in high enough numbers, they may appear as a green discoloration of the water due to the presence of chlorophyll within their cells.
Biomass	Biomass, in the energy production industry, refers to living and recently dead biological material which can be used as fuel or for industrial production. Most commonly, biomass refers to plant matter grown for use as biofuel, but it also includes plant or animal matter used for production of fibres, chemicals or heat. Biomass may also include biodegradable wastes that can be burnt as fuel. It excludes organic material which has been transformed by geological processes into substances such as coal or petroleum.
Eutrophication	Eutrophication refers to an increase in the primary productivity of any ecosystem. Eutrophication is caused by the increase of chemical nutrients, typically compounds containing nitrogen or phosphorus. It may occur on land or in water.
Frequency	Frequency is the measurement of the number of occurrences of a repeated event per unit of time. It is also defined as the rate of change of phase of a sinusoidal waveform.
Sediment	Sediment is any particulate matter that can be transported by fluid flow and which eventually is deposited as a layer of solid particles on the bed or bottom of a body of water or other liquid.
Benthos	Benthos are the organisms which live on, in, or near the seabed. Although the term derived from the Greek for "depths of the sea", the term is also used in freshwater biology to refer to organisms at the bottoms of freshwater bodies of water, such as lakes, rivers, and streams.

Go to **Cram101.com** for the Practice Tests for this Chapter.
And, **NEVER** highlight a book again!

Attenuation	Attenuation is the reduction in amplitude and intensity of a signal.
Radiation	Radiation as used in physics, is energy in the form of waves or moving subatomic particles.
Primary production	Primary production is the production of organic compounds from atmospheric or aquatic carbon dioxide, principally through the process of photosynthesis, with chemosynthesis being much less important. All life on earth is directly or indirectly reliant on it.
Equilibrium	Equilibrium is the condition of a system in which competing influences are balanced.
Aquatic	The term aquatic refers to water and can be either a noun or an adjective. Dictionary definitions do not specify what kind of water, although in both general use and in the sciences, the implication is often that of fresh water.
Amplitude	The amplitude is a nonnegative scalar measure of a wave's magnitude of oscillation, that is, the magnitude of the maximum disturbance in the medium during one wave cycle. When amplitude of sound wave changes, a listener would hear a change in pitch.
Lake	A lake is a body of water or other liquid of considerable size contained on a body of land. A vast majority are fresh water, and lie in the Northern Hemisphere at higher latitudes. Most have a natural outflow in the form of a river or stream, but some do not, and lose water solely by evaporation and/or underground seepage.
Chlorophyll	Chlorophyll is a green pigment found in most plants, algae, and cyanobacteria.
Plankton	Plankton are any drifting organism that inhabits the water column of oceans, seas, and bodies of fresh water. They are widely considered to be some of the most important organisms on Earth, due to the food supply they provide to most aquatic life.

Sediment	Sediment is any particulate matter that can be transported by fluid flow and which eventually is deposited as a layer of solid particles on the bed or bottom of a body of water or other liquid.
Oxide	An oxide is a chemical compound containing an oxygen atom and other elements. Most of the earth's crust consists of them. They result when elements are oxidized by air.
Matter	Matter is the substance of which physical objects are composed. Matter can be solid, liquid, plasma or gas. It constitutes the observable universe.
Benthos	Benthos are the organisms which live on, in, or near the seabed. Although the term derived from the Greek for "depths of the sea", the term is also used in freshwater biology to refer to organisms at the bottoms of freshwater bodies of water, such as lakes, rivers, and streams.
Nonpoint sources	Nonpoint sources comes from many unidentifiable sources with no specific solution to rectify the proble, making it difficult to regulate. An example would be urban runnoff of items like oil, fertilizers, and lawn chemicals. As rainfall or snowmelt moves over and through the ground, it picks up and carries away natural and human-made pollutants.
Closed system	In thermodynamics, a closed system can exchange heat and work, but not matter, with its surroundings.
Thermal	A thermal column is a column of rizing air in the lower altitudes of the Earth face=symbol>¢s atmosphere. Thermals are created by the uneven heating of the Earth's surface from solar radiation, and are an example of convection. The Sun warms the ground, which in turn warms the air directly above it.
Thermocline	The thermocline is a layer within a body of water or air where the temperature changes rapidly with depth.
Organism	In biology and ecology, an organism is a living complex adaptive system of organs that influence each other in such a way that they function in some way as a stable whole.
Bacteria	Bacteria are unicellular microorganisms. They are typically a few micrometres long and have many shapes including curved rods, spheres, rods, and spirals.
Mineral	A mineral is a naturally occurring substance formed through geological processes that has a characteristic chemical composition, a highly ordered atomic structure and specific physical properties. A rock, by comparison, is an aggregate of minerals and need not have a specific chemical composition. Minerals range in composition from pure elements and simple salts to very complex silicates with thousands of known forms.
Mollusks	The mollusks are members of the large and diverse phylum, which includes a variety of familiar animals well-known for their decorative shells or as seafood. These range from tiny snails, clams, and abalone to larger organisms such as squid, cuttlefish and the octopus
Lake	A lake is a body of water or other liquid of considerable size contained on a body of land. A vast majority are fresh water, and lie in the Northern Hemisphere at higher latitudes. Most have a natural outflow in the form of a river or stream, but some do not, and lose water solely by evaporation and/or underground seepage.
Phytoplankton	Phytoplankton are the autotrophic component of plankton. Most phytoplankton are too small to be individually seen with the unaided eye. However, when present in high enough numbers, they may appear as a green discoloration of the water due to the presence of chlorophyll within their cells.
Chlorophyll	Chlorophyll is a green pigment found in most plants, algae, and cyanobacteria.

Metabolism	Metabolism is the complete set of chemical reactions that occur in living cells. These processes are the basis of life, allowing cells to grow and reproduce, maintain their structures, and respond to their environments.
Eutrophication	Eutrophication refers to an increase in the primary productivity of any ecosystem. Eutrophication is caused by the increase of chemical nutrients, typically compounds containing nitrogen or phosphorus. It may occur on land or in water.
Aerobic	An aerobic organism is an organism that has an oxygen based metabolism
Diffusion	Diffusion is the net action of matter, particles or molecules, heat, momentum, or light whose end is to minimize a concentration gradient.
Denitrification	Denitrification is the process of reducing nitrate and nitrite, highly oxidised forms of nitrogen available for consumption by many groups of organisms, into gaseous nitrogen, which is far less accessible to life forms but makes up the bulk of our atmosphere. The process is performed by heterotrophic bacteria from all main proteolytic groups.
Buoyancy	In physics, buoyancy is the upward force on an object produced by the surrounding fluid in which it is fully or partially immersed, due to the pressure difference of the fluid between the top and bottom of the object. The net upward buoyancy force is equal to the magnitude of the weight of fluid displaced by the body.
Ion	An ion is an atom or group of atoms which have lost or gained one or more electrons, making them negatively or positively charged.
Competition	Competition between members of a species is the driving force behind evolution and natural selection; especially for resources such as food, water, territory, and sunlight results in the ultimate survival and dominance of the variation of the species best suited for survival.
Biomass	Biomass, in the energy production industry, refers to living and recently dead biological material which can be used as fuel or for industrial production. Most commonly, biomass refers to plant matter grown for use as biofuel, but it also includes plant or animal matter used for production of fibres, chemicals or heat. Biomass may also include biodegradable wastes that can be burnt as fuel. It excludes organic material which has been transformed by geological processes into substances such as coal or petroleum.
Phosphate	A phosphate, in inorganic chemistry, is a salt of phosphoric acid. In organic chemistry it is an ester of phosphoric acid.
Particulates	Particulates are tiny particles of solid or liquid suspended in a gas. They range in size from less than 10 nanometres to more than 100 micrometres in diameter.
Porosity	Porosity is a measure of the void spaces in a material, and is measured as a fraction, between 0–1, or as a percentage between 0–100%.
Island	An island is any piece of land that is completely surrounded by water, above high tide. There are two main types of islands: continental islands and oceanic islands. There are also artificial islands. A grouping of geographically and/or geologically related islands is called an archipelago.
Precipitation	Precipitation is any product of the condensation of atmospheric water vapor that is deposited on the earth's surface. It occurs when the atmosphere becomes saturated with water vapour and the water condenses and falls out of solution. Air becomes saturated via two processes, cooling and adding moisture.
Residence time	Residence time is a broadly useful concept that expresses how fast something moves through a system in equilibrium. It is the average time a substance spends within a specified region of space, such as a reservoir.

Go to **Cram101.com** for the Practice Tests for this Chapter.

Stream	A stream is a body of water with a current, confined within a bed and banks. Streams are important as conduits in the water cycle, instruments in aquifer recharge, and corridors for fish and wildlife migration.
Photosynthesis	Photosynthesis generally, is the synthesis of triose phosphates from sunlight, carbon dioxide and water.
Bacteria	Bacteria are unicellular microorganisms. They are typically a few micrometres long and have many shapes including curved rods, spheres, rods, and spirals.
Biochemical oxygen demand	Biochemical oxygen demand is a chemical procedure for determining how fast biological organisms use up oxygen in a body of water.
Algae	Algae encompass several groups of relatively simple living aquatic organisms that capture light energy through photosynthesis, using it to convert inorganic substances into organic matter.
Chlorophyll	Chlorophyll is a green pigment found in most plants, algae, and cyanobacteria.
Sediment	Sediment is any particulate matter that can be transported by fluid flow and which eventually is deposited as a layer of solid particles on the bed or bottom of a body of water or other liquid.
Benthos	Benthos are the organisms which live on, in, or near the seabed. Although the term derived from the Greek for "depths of the sea", the term is also used in freshwater biology to refer to organisms at the bottoms of freshwater bodies of water, such as lakes, rivers, and streams.
Diurnal	A diurnal animal is an animal that is active during the daytime and rests during the night.
Mineral	A mineral is a naturally occurring substance formed through geological processes that has a characteristic chemical composition, a highly ordered atomic structure and specific physical properties. A rock, by comparison, is an aggregate of minerals and need not have a specific chemical composition. Minerals range in composition from pure elements and simple salts to very complex silicates with thousands of known forms.
Phosphorus cycle	The phosphorus cycle is the biogeochemical cycle that describes the movement of phosphorus through the lithosphere, hydrosphere, and biosphere.
Nitrogen	Nitrogen is a chemical element which has the symbol N and atomic number 7. Elemental nitrogen is a colorless, odourless, tasteless and mostly inert diatomic gas at standard conditions, constituting 78.1% by volume of Earth's atmosphere.
Nitrogen cycle	The nitrogen cycle is the biogeochemical cycle that describes the transformations of nitrogen and nitrogen-containing compounds in nature.
Latitude	Latitude gives the location of a place on Earth north or south of the equator. Lines of Latitude are the horizontal lines shown running east-to-west on maps. Technically, Latitude is an angular measurement in degrees ranging from 0° at the Equator to 90° at the poles.
Longitude	Longitude is the east-west geographic coordinate measurement most commonly utilized in cartography and global navigation.
Attenuation	Attenuation is the reduction in amplitude and intensity of a signal.
Eutrophication	Eutrophication refers to an increase in the primary productivity of any ecosystem. Eutrophication is caused by the increase of chemical nutrients, typically compounds containing nitrogen or phosphorus. It may occur on land or in water.

Bacteria	Bacteria are unicellular microorganisms. They are typically a few micrometres long and have many shapes including curved rods, spheres, rods, and spirals.
Interference	Interference is the addition of two or more waves that results in a new wave pattern. As most commonly used, the term interference usually refers to the interaction of waves which are correlated or coherent with each other, either because they come from the same source or because they have the same or nearly the same frequency.
Water pollution	Water pollution is a large set of adverse effects upon water bodies such as lakes, rivers, oceans, and groundwater caused by human activities. Although natural phenomena such as volcanoes, algae blooms, storms, and earthquakes also cause major changes in water quality and the ecological status of water, these are not deemed to be pollution. Water pollution has many causes and characteristics.
Pollution	Pollution is the introduction of substances or energy into the environment, resulting in deleterious effects of such a nature as to endanger human health, harm living resources and ecosystems, and impair or interfere with amenities and other legitimate uses of the environment.
Pathogen	A pathogen is a biological agent that causes disease or illness to its host.
Chlorophyll	Chlorophyll is a green pigment found in most plants, algae, and cyanobacteria.
Protein	Protein is a large organic compounds made of amino acids arranged in a linear chain and joined together by peptide bonds between the carboxyl and amino groups of adjacent amino acid residues. The sequence of amino acids in a protein is defined by a gene and encoded in the genetic code.
Algae	Algae encompass several groups of relatively simple living aquatic organisms that capture light energy through photosynthesis, using it to convert inorganic substances into organic matter.
Storm	A storm is any disturbed state of an astronomical body's atmosphere, especially affecting its surface, and strongly implying severe weather. It may be marked by strong wind, thunder and lightning, heavy precipitation, such as ice, or wind transporting some substance through the atmosphere.
Radiation	Radiation as used in physics, is energy in the form of waves or moving subatomic particles.
Salinity	Salinity is the saltiness or dissolved salt content of a body of water. In oceanography, it has been traditional to express halinity not as percent, but as parts per thousand, which is approximately grams of salt per liter of solution.
Extinction	In biology and ecology, extinction is the cessation of existence of a species or group of taxa, reducing biodiversity. The moment of extinction is generally considered to be the death of the last individual of that species.
Particulates	Particulates are tiny particles of solid or liquid suspended in a gas. They range in size from less than 10 nanometres to more than 100 micrometres in diameter.
Matter	Matter is the substance of which physical objects are composed. Matter can be solid, liquid, plasma or gas. It constitutes the observable universe.
Equilibrium	Equilibrium is the condition of a system in which competing influences are balanced.
Stream	A stream is a body of water with a current, confined within a bed and banks. Streams are important as conduits in the water cycle, instruments in aquifer recharge, and corridors for fish and wildlife migration.
Weather	The weather is the set of all extant phenomena in a given atmosphere at a given time. The term usually refers to the activity of these phenomena over short periods, as opposed to the

term climate, which refers to the average atmospheric conditions over longer periods of time.

Residence time	Residence time is a broadly useful concept that expresses how fast something moves through a system in equilibrium. It is the average time a substance spends within a specified region of space, such as a reservoir.
Surface water	Water collecting on the ground or in a stream, river, lake, or wetland is called surface water; as opposed to groundwater. Surface water is naturally replenished by precipitation and naturally lost through discharge to the oceans, evaporation, and sub-surface seepage into the groundwater. Surface water is the largest source of fresh water.
Lake	A lake is a body of water or other liquid of considerable size contained on a body of land. A vast majority are fresh water, and lie in the Northern Hemisphere at higher latitudes. Most have a natural outflow in the form of a river or stream, but some do not, and lose water solely by evaporation and/or underground seepage.
Sediment	Sediment is any particulate matter that can be transported by fluid flow and which eventually is deposited as a layer of solid particles on the bed or bottom of a body of water or other liquid.
Organism	In biology and ecology, an organism is a living complex adaptive system of organs that influence each other in such a way that they function in some way as a stable whole.
Nonpoint sources	Nonpoint sources comes from many unidentifiable sources with no specific solution to rectify the proble, making it difficult to regulate. An example would be urban runoff of items like oil, fertilizers, and lawn chemicals. As rainfall or snowmelt moves over and through the ground, it picks up and carries away natural and human-made pollutants.
Forest	A forest is an area with a high density of trees, historically, a wooded area set aside for hunting. These plant communities cover large areas of the globe and function as animal habitats, hydrologic flow modulators, and soil conservers, constituting one of the most important aspects of the Earth's biosphere.
Potable water	Water of sufficient quality to serve as drinking water is termed potable water whether it is used as such or not.
Thermocline	The thermocline is a layer within a body of water or air where the temperature changes rapidly with depth.
Diffusion	Diffusion is the net action of matter, particles or molecules, heat, momentum, or light whose end is to minimize a concentration gradient.
Viscosity	Viscosity is a measure of the resistance of a fluid to deform under shear stress. It is commonly perceived as "thickness", or resistance to flow. Viscosity describes a fluid face=symbol>¢s internal resistance to flow and may be thought of as a measure of fluid friction.

Eutrophication	Eutrophication refers to an increase in the primary productivity of any ecosystem. Eutrophication is caused by the increase of chemical nutrients, typically compounds containing nitrogen or phosphorus. It may occur on land or in water.
Aquatic	The term aquatic refers to water and can be either a noun or an adjective. Dictionary definitions do not specify what kind of water, although in both general use and in the sciences, the implication is often that of fresh water.
Thermal	A thermal column is a column of rizing air in the lower altitudes of the Earth face=symbol>¢s atmosphere. Thermals are created by the uneven heating of the Earth's surface from solar radiation, and are an example of convection. The Sun warms the ground, which in turn warms the air directly above it.
Algae	Algae encompass several groups of relatively simple living aquatic organisms that capture light energy through photosynthesis, using it to convert inorganic substances into organic matter.
Bacteria	Bacteria are unicellular microorganisms. They are typically a few micrometres long and have many shapes including curved rods, spheres, rods, and spirals.
Photosynthesis	Photosynthesis generally, is the synthesis of triose phosphates from sunlight, carbon dioxide and water.
Stream	A stream is a body of water with a current, confined within a bed and banks. Streams are important as conduits in the water cycle, instruments in aquifer recharge, and corridors for fish and wildlife migration.
Drainage	Drainage is the natural or artificial removal of surface and sub-surface water from a given area. Many agricultural soils need drainage to improve production or to manage water supplies.
Drainage basin	A drainage basin is a region of land where water from rain or snow melt drains downhill into a body of water, such as a river, lake, dam, estuary, wetland, sea or ocean. The drainage basin includes both the streams and rivers that convey the water as well as the land surfaces from which water drains into those channels. The drainage basin acts like a funnel - collecting all the water within the area covered by the basin and channeling it into a waterway.
Lake	A lake is a body of water or other liquid of considerable size contained on a body of land. A vast majority are fresh water, and lie in the Northern Hemisphere at higher latitudes. Most have a natural outflow in the form of a river or stream, but some do not, and lose water solely by evaporation and/or underground seepage.
Marsh	In geography, a marsh is a type of wetland which is subject to almost continuous inundation. Typically it features grasses, rushes, reeds, typhas, sedges, and other herbaceous plants in a context of shallow water. It is different from a swamp, which has a greater proportion of open water surface, and is generally deeper than a it.
Cultural eutrophication	Cultural eutrophication is the process that speeds up natural eutrophication because of human activity. Due to clearing of land and building of towns and cities, run - off water is accelerated and more nutrients such as phosphates and nitrate are supplied to the lakes and ponds
Oligotrophic	Oligotrophic refers to any environment that offers little to sustain life. This term is usually used to describe bodies of water or soils with very low nutrient levels.
Carbon	Carbon is a chemical element. An abundant nonmetallic, tetravalent element, carbon has several allotropic forms. This element is the basis of the chemistry of all known life.
Carbon dioxide	Carbon dioxide is a chemical compound, normally in a gaseous state, and is composed of one

Go to **Cram101.com** for the Practice Tests for this Chapter.

carbon and two oxygen atoms. It is often referred to by its formula CO2. It is present in the Earth's atmosphere at a concentration of approximately .000383 by
volume and is an important greenhouse gas due to its ability to absorb many infrared wavelengths of sunlight, and due to the length of time it stays in the atmosphere.

Ecosystem	An ecosystem is a natural unit consisting of all plants, animals and micro organisms in an area functioning together with all the non living physical factors of the environment.
Biomass	Biomass, in the energy production industry, refers to living and recently dead biological material which can be used as fuel or for industrial production. Most commonly, biomass refers to plant matter grown for use as biofuel, but it also includes plant or animal matter used for production of fibres, chemicals or heat. Biomass may also include biodegradable wastes that can be burnt as fuel. It excludes organic material which has been transformed by geological processes into substances such as coal or petroleum.
Silica	Silica is the oxide of silicon, chemical formula SiO_2, and is known for its hardness as early as the 16th century. It is a principle component in most types of glass and substances such as concrete.
Crust	In geology, a crust is the outermost layer of a planet, part of its lithosphere. They are generally composed of a less dense material than its deeper layers.Earths face=symbol>¢ is composed mainly of basalt and granite. It is cooler and more rigid than the deeper layers of the mantle and core.
Phosphate	A phosphate, in inorganic chemistry, is a salt of phosphoric acid. In organic chemistry it is an ester of phosphoric acid.
Sediment	Sediment is any particulate matter that can be transported by fluid flow and which eventually is deposited as a layer of solid particles on the bed or bottom of a body of water or other liquid.
Nonpoint sources	Nonpoint sources comes from many unidentifiable sources with no specific solution to rectify the proble, making it difficult to regulate. An example would be urban runnoff of items like oil, fertilizers, and lawn chemicals. As rainfall or snowmelt moves over and through the ground, it picks up and carries away natural and human-made pollutants.
Erosion	Erosion is displacement of solids by the agents of ocean currents, wind, water, or ice by downward or down-slope movement in response to gravity or by living organisms.
Detritus	In biology, detritus is non-living particulate organic material. It typically includes the bodies of dead organisms or fragments of organisms or faecal material. Detritus is normally colonised by communities of microorganisms which act to decompose the material.
Matter	Matter is the substance of which physical objects are composed. Matter can be solid, liquid, plasma or gas. It constitutes the observable universe.
Phytoplankton	Phytoplankton are the autotrophic component of plankton. Most phytoplankton are too small to be individually seen with the unaided eye. However, when present in high enough numbers, they may appear as a green discoloration of the water due to the presence of chlorophyll within their cells.
Zooplankton	Zooplankton are the heterotrophic component of the plankton that drift in the water column of oceans, seas, and bodies of fresh water. Many zooplankton are too small to be individually seen with the unaided eye.
Nitrogen	Nitrogen is a chemical element which has the symbol N and atomic number 7. Elemental nitrogen is a colorless, odourless, tasteless and mostly inert diatomic gas at standard conditions, constituting 78.1% by volume of Earth's atmosphere.
Nitrogen cycle	The nitrogen cycle is the biogeochemical cycle that describes the transformations of nitrogen

and nitrogen-containing compounds in nature.

Oxide	An oxide is a chemical compound containing an oxygen atom and other elements. Most of the earth's crust consists of them. They result when elements are oxidized by air.
Aerobic	An aerobic organism is an organism that has an oxygen based metabolism
Aerobic bacteria	An aerobic bacteria is an organism that has an oxygen based metabolism. Aerobes, in a process known as cellular respiration, use oxygen to oxidize substrates in order to obtain energy.
Denitrification	Denitrification is the process of reducing nitrate and nitrite, highly oxidised forms of nitrogen available for consumption by many groups of organisms, into gaseous nitrogen, which is far less accessible to life forms but makes up the bulk of our atmosphere. The process is performed by heterotrophic bacteria from all main proteolytic groups.
Electron	The electron is a fundamental subatomic particle that carries a negative electric charge.
Nitrogen fixation	Nitrogen fixation is the process by which nitrogen is taken from its relatively inert molecular form in the atmosphere and converted into nitrogen compounds, useful for other chemical processes.
Particulates	Particulates are tiny particles of solid or liquid suspended in a gas. They range in size from less than 10 nanometres to more than 100 micrometres in diameter.
Groundwater	Groundwater is water located beneath the ground surface in soil pore spaces and in the fractures of geologic formations. Groundwater is recharged from, and eventually flows to, the surface naturally; natural discharge often occurs at springs and seeps, streams and can often form oases or wetlands.
Primary production	Primary production is the production of organic compounds from atmospheric or aquatic carbon dioxide, principally through the process of photosynthesis, with chemosynthesis being much less important. All life on earth is directly or indirectly reliant on it.
Pollution	Pollution is the introduction of substances or energy into the environment, resulting in deleterious effects of such a nature as to endanger human health, harm living resources and ecosystems, and impair or interfere with amenities and other legitimate uses of the environment.
Carbon cycle	The carbon cycle is the biogeochemical cycle by which carbon is exchanged between the biosphere, geosphere, hydrosphere, and atmosphere of the Earth.
Diatoms	Diatoms are a major group of eukaryotic algae, and are one of the most common types of phytoplankton. Most diatoms are unicellular, although some form chains or simple colonies. A characteristic feature of diatom cells is that they are encased within a unique cell wall made of silica called a frustule.
Island	An island is any piece of land that is completely surrounded by water, above high tide. There are two main types of islands: continental islands and oceanic islands. There are also artificial islands. A grouping of geographically and/or geologically related islands is called an archipelago.
Food web	Food web refers to describe the feeding relationships between species in an ecological community. Typically a food web refers to a graph where only connections are recorded, and a food web or ecosystem network refers to a network where the connections are given weights representing the quantity of nutrients or energy being transferred.
Chlorophyll	Chlorophyll is a green pigment found in most plants, algae, and cyanobacteria.
Radiation	Radiation as used in physics, is energy in the form of waves or moving subatomic particles.

Go to Cram101.com for the Practice Tests for this Chapter.

Forest	A forest is an area with a high density of trees, historically, a wooded area set aside for hunting. These plant communities cover large areas of the globe and function as animal habitats, hydrologic flow modulators, and soil conservers, constituting one of the most important aspects of the Earth's biosphere.
Residence time	Residence time is a broadly useful concept that expresses how fast something moves through a system in equilibrium. It is the average time a substance spends within a specified region of space, such as a reservoir.

Go to **Cram101.com** for the Practice Tests for this Chapter.

Lake	A lake is a body of water or other liquid of considerable size contained on a body of land. A vast majority are fresh water, and lie in the Northern Hemisphere at higher latitudes. Most have a natural outflow in the form of a river or stream, but some do not, and lose water solely by evaporation and/or underground seepage.
Ion	An ion is an atom or group of atoms which have lost or gained one or more electrons, making them negatively or positively charged.
Eutrophication	Eutrophication refers to an increase in the primary productivity of any ecosystem. Eutrophication is caused by the increase of chemical nutrients, typically compounds containing nitrogen or phosphorus. It may occur on land or in water.
Oligotrophic	Oligotrophic refers to any environment that offers little to sustain life. This term is usually used to describe bodies of water or soils with very low nutrient levels.
Residence time	Residence time is a broadly useful concept that expresses how fast something moves through a system in equilibrium. It is the average time a substance spends within a specified region of space, such as a reservoir.
Chlorophyll	Chlorophyll is a green pigment found in most plants, algae, and cyanobacteria.
Extinction	In biology and ecology, extinction is the cessation of existence of a species or group of taxa, reducing biodiversity. The moment of extinction is generally considered to be the death of the last individual of that species.
Sverdrup	The sverdrup is a unit of measure of volume transport. It is used almost exclusively in oceanography, to measure the transport of ocean currents. It is equivalent to 106 cubic meters per second.
Sediment	Sediment is any particulate matter that can be transported by fluid flow and which eventually is deposited as a layer of solid particles on the bed or bottom of a body of water or other liquid.
Dredging	Dredging is an excavation activity or operation usually carried out at least partly underwater, in shallow seas or fresh water areas with the purpose of gathering up bottom sediments and disposing of them at a different location.
Recycling	Recycling is the reprocessing of materials into new products. It prevents useful material resources being wasted, reduces the consumption of raw materials and reduces energy usage, and hence greenhouse gas emissions, compared to virgin production.
Thermocline	The thermocline is a layer within a body of water or air where the temperature changes rapidly with depth.
Photosynthesis	Photosynthesis generally, is the synthesis of triose phosphates from sunlight, carbon dioxide and water.
Matter	Matter is the substance of which physical objects are composed. Matter can be solid, liquid, plasma or gas. It constitutes the observable universe.
Particulates	Particulates are tiny particles of solid or liquid suspended in a gas. They range in size from less than 10 nanometres to more than 100 micrometres in diameter.
Surface water	Water collecting on the ground or in a stream, river, lake, or wetland is called surface water; as opposed to groundwater. Surface water is naturally replenished by precipitation and naturally lost through discharge to the oceans, evaporation, and sub-surface seepage into the groundwater. Surface water is the largest source of fresh water.
Phytoplankton	Phytoplankton are the autotrophic component of plankton. Most phytoplankton are too small to be individually seen with the unaided eye. However, when present in high enough numbers, they may appear as a green discoloration of the water due to the presence of chlorophyll within

	their cells.
Island	An island is any piece of land that is completely surrounded by water, above high tide. There are two main types of islands: continental islands and oceanic islands. There are also artificial islands. A grouping of geographically and/or geologically related islands is called an archipelago.
Thermal	A thermal column is a column of rizing air in the lower altitudes of the Earth face=symbol>¢s atmosphere. Thermals are created by the uneven heating of the Earth's surface from solar radiation, and are an example of convection. The Sun warms the ground, which in turn warms the air directly above it.
Diffusion	Diffusion is the net action of matter, particles or molecules, heat, momentum, or light whose end is to minimize a concentration gradient.
Zooplankton	Zooplankton are the heterotrophic component of the plankton that drift in the water column of oceans, seas, and bodies of fresh water. Many zooplankton are too small to be individually seen with the unaided eye.
Gravel	Gravel is rock that is of a certain particle size range. In geology, gravel is any loose rock that is at least two millimeters in its largest dimension and no more than 75 millimeters.
Groundwater	Groundwater is water located beneath the ground surface in soil pore spaces and in the fractures of geologic formations. Groundwater is recharged from, and eventually flows to, the surface naturally; natural discharge often occurs at springs and seeps, streams and can often form oases or wetlands.
Evaporation	Evaporation is the process by which molecules in a liquid state become a gas.
Precipitation	Precipitation is any product of the condensation of atmospheric water vapor that is deposited on the earth's surface. It occurs when the atmosphere becomes saturated with water vapour and the water condenses and falls out of solution. Air becomes saturated via two processes, cooling and adding moisture.
Porosity	Porosity is a measure of the void spaces in a material, and is measured as a fraction, between 0–1, or as a percentage between 0–100%.

Lake	A lake is a body of water or other liquid of considerable size contained on a body of land. A vast majority are fresh water, and lie in the Northern Hemisphere at higher latitudes. Most have a natural outflow in the form of a river or stream, but some do not, and lose water solely by evaporation and/or underground seepage.
Thermal	A thermal column is a column of rizing air in the lower altitudes of the Earth face=symbol>¢s atmosphere. Thermals are created by the uneven heating of the Earth's surface from solar radiation, and are an example of convection. The Sun warms the ground, which in turn warms the air directly above it.
Diurnal	A diurnal animal is an animal that is active during the daytime and rests during the night.
Channelization	Channelization secures a definite available depth for navigation; and the discharge of the river generally is amply sufficient for maintaining the impounded waterlevel, as well as providing the necessary water for locking.
Toxicity	Toxicity is a measure of the degree to which something is toxic or poisonous. Toxicity can refer to the effect on a whole organism, such as a human or a bacterium or a plant, or to a substructure, such as a cell or an organ.
Eutrophication	Eutrophication refers to an increase in the primary productivity of any ecosystem. Eutrophication is caused by the increase of chemical nutrients, typically compounds containing nitrogen or phosphorus. It may occur on land or in water.
Atmosphere	An atmosphere is a layer of gases that may surround a material body of sufficient mass. The gases are attracted by the gravity of the body, and are retained for a longer duration if gravity is high and the atmosphere's temperature is low. Some planets consist mainly of various gases, and thus have very deep atmospheres.
Nonpoint sources	Nonpoint sources comes from many unidentifiable sources with no specific solution to rectify the proble, making it difficult to regulate. An example would be urban runoff of items like oil, fertilizers, and lawn chemicals. As rainfall or snowmelt moves over and through the ground, it picks up and carries away natural and human-made pollutants.
Stream	A stream is a body of water with a current, confined within a bed and banks. Streams are important as conduits in the water cycle, instruments in aquifer recharge, and corridors for fish and wildlife migration.
Radiation	Radiation as used in physics, is energy in the form of waves or moving subatomic particles.
Evaporation	Evaporation is the process by which molecules in a liquid state become a gas.
Convection	Convection in the most general terms refers to the movement of currents within fluids. Convection is one of the major modes of Heat and mass transfer. In fluids, convective heat and mass transfer take place through both diffusion and by advection, in which matter or heat is transported by the larger-scale motion of currents in the fluid.
Condensation	Condensation is the change in matter of a substance to a denser phase, such as a gas to a liquid. Condensation commonly occurs when a vapor is cooled to a liquid, but can also occur if a vapor is compressed into a liquid, or undergoes a combination of cooling and compression.
Matter	Matter is the substance of which physical objects are composed. Matter can be solid, liquid, plasma or gas. It constitutes the observable universe.
Wavelength	In physics, wavelength is the distance between repeating units of a propagating wave of a given frequency. It is commonly designated by the Greek letter lambda. Examples of wave-like phenomena are light, water waves, and sound waves. Wavelength of a sine wave.In a wave, a property varies with the position.

Go to **Cram101.com** for the Practice Tests for this Chapter.

Relative humidity	Relative humidity is a term used to describe the quantity of water vapor that exists in a gaseous mixture of air and water.
Humidity	Humidity is a term used to describe the amount of water vapor in air. Absolute humidity, relative humidity, and specific humidity are different ways to express the water content in a parcel of air.
Dew	Dew is water in the form of droplets that appears on thin, exposed objects in the morning or evening. As the exposed surface cools by radiating its heat, atmospheric moisture condenses at a rate greater than that of which it can evaporate, resulting in the formation of water droplets.
Precipitation	Precipitation is any product of the condensation of atmospheric water vapor that is deposited on the earth's surface. It occurs when the atmosphere becomes saturated with water vapour and the water condenses and falls out of solution. Air becomes saturated via two processes, cooling and adding moisture.
Surface water	Water collecting on the ground or in a stream, river, lake, or wetland is called surface water; as opposed to groundwater. Surface water is naturally replenished by precipitation and naturally lost through discharge to the oceans, evaporation, and sub-surface seepage into the groundwater. Surface water is the largest source of fresh water.
Altitude	Altitude is the elevation of an object from a known level or datum. Common datums are mean sea level and the surface of the World Geodetic System geoid, used by Global Positioning System. In aviation, altitude is measured in feet. For non-aviation uses, altitude may be measured in other units such as metres or miles.
Latitude	Latitude gives the location of a place on Earth north or south of the equator. Lines of Latitude are the horizontal lines shown running east-to-west on maps. Technically, Latitude is an angular measurement in degrees ranging from 0° at the Equator to 90° at the poles.
Albedo	The albedo of an object is the extent to which it reflects light, defined as the ratio of reflected to incident electromagnetic radiation. It is a unitless measure indicative of a surface's or body's diffuse reflectivity.
Attenuation	Attenuation is the reduction in amplitude and intensity of a signal.
Molecule	In chemistry, a molecule is defined as a sufficiently stable electrically neutral group of at least two atoms in a definite arrangement held together by strong chemical bonds.
Equilibrium	Equilibrium is the condition of a system in which competing influences are balanced.

Go to **Cram101.com** for the Practice Tests for this Chapter.

Thermal	A thermal column is a column of rizing air in the lower altitudes of the Earth face=symbol>¢s atmosphere. Thermals are created by the uneven heating of the Earth's surface from solar radiation, and are an example of convection. The Sun warms the ground, which in turn warms the air directly above it.
Lake	A lake is a body of water or other liquid of considerable size contained on a body of land. A vast majority are fresh water, and lie in the Northern Hemisphere at higher latitudes. Most have a natural outflow in the form of a river or stream, but some do not, and lose water solely by evaporation and/or underground seepage.
Eutrophication	Eutrophication refers to an increase in the primary productivity of any ecosystem. Eutrophication is caused by the increase of chemical nutrients, typically compounds containing nitrogen or phosphorus. It may occur on land or in water.
Pollution	Pollution is the introduction of substances or energy into the environment, resulting in deleterious effects of such a nature as to endanger human health, harm living resources and ecosystems, and impair or interfere with amenities and other legitimate uses of the environment.
Gravitation	Gravitation, in everyday life, is most familiar as the agency that endows objects with weight. Gravitation is responsible for keeping the Earth and the other planets in their orbits around the Sun; for the formation of tides; and for various other phenomena that we observe. Gravitation is also the reason for the very existence of the Earth, the Sun, and most macroscopic objects in the universe; without it, matter would not have coalesced into these large masses, and life, as we know it, would not exist.
Radiation	Radiation as used in physics, is energy in the form of waves or moving subatomic particles.
Relative humidity	Relative humidity is a term used to describe the quantity of water vapor that exists in a gaseous mixture of air and water.
Humidity	Humidity is a term used to describe the amount of water vapor in air. Absolute humidity, relative humidity, and specific humidity are different ways to express the water content in a parcel of air.
Buoyancy	In physics, buoyancy is the upward force on an object produced by the surrounding fluid in which it is fully or partially immersed, due to the pressure difference of the fluid between the top and bottom of the object. The net upward buoyancy force is equal to the magnitude of the weight of fluid displaced by the body.
Thermocline	The thermocline is a layer within a body of water or air where the temperature changes rapidly with depth.
Convection	Convection in the most general terms refers to the movement of currents within fluids. Convection is one of the major modes of Heat and mass transfer. In fluids, convective heat and mass transfer take place through both diffusion and by advection, in which matter or heat is transported by the larger-scale motion of currents in the fluid.
Surface water	Water collecting on the ground or in a stream, river, lake, or wetland is called surface water; as opposed to groundwater. Surface water is naturally replenished by precipitation and naturally lost through discharge to the oceans, evaporation, and sub-surface seepage into the groundwater. Surface water is the largest source of fresh water.
Diffusion	Diffusion is the net action of matter, particles or molecules, heat, momentum, or light whose end is to minimize a concentration gradient.
Phytoplankton	Phytoplankton are the autotrophic component of plankton. Most phytoplankton are too small to be individually seen with the unaided eye. However, when present in high enough numbers, they may appear as a green discoloration of the water due to the presence of chlorophyll within

	their cells.
Sediment	Sediment is any particulate matter that can be transported by fluid flow and which eventually is deposited as a layer of solid particles on the bed or bottom of a body of water or other liquid.
Oligotrophic	Oligotrophic refers to any environment that offers little to sustain life. This term is usually used to describe bodies of water or soils with very low nutrient levels.
Eutrophic lake	A eutrophic lake is a lake with high primary productivity, the result of high nutrient content. These lakes are subject to excessive algal blooms, resulting in murky water and poor water quality. The bottom waters of such lakes are commonly deficient in oxygen.
Extinction	In biology and ecology, extinction is the cessation of existence of a species or group of taxa, reducing biodiversity. The moment of extinction is generally considered to be the death of the last individual of that species.
Island	An island is any piece of land that is completely surrounded by water, above high tide. There are two main types of islands: continental islands and oceanic islands. There are also artificial islands. A grouping of geographically and/or geologically related islands is called an archipelago.
Kinetic energy	The kinetic energy of an object is the extra energy which it possesses due to its motion. It is defined as the work needed to accelerate a body of a given mass from rest to its current velocity. Term or phrase NOT in the knowledge-core.

Go to **Cram101.com** for the Practice Tests for this Chapter.

Microorganism	A microorganism is an organism that is microscopic. They can be bacteria, fungi, archaea or protists, but not viruses and prions, which are generally classified as non-living. Micro-organisms are generally single-celled, or unicellular organisms.
Bacteria	Bacteria are unicellular microorganisms. They are typically a few micrometres long and have many shapes including curved rods, spheres, rods, and spirals.
Pathogen	A pathogen is a biological agent that causes disease or illness to its host.
Eutrophication	Eutrophication refers to an increase in the primary productivity of any ecosystem. Eutrophication is caused by the increase of chemical nutrients, typically compounds containing nitrogen or phosphorus. It may occur on land or in water.
Biomass	Biomass, in the energy production industry, refers to living and recently dead biological material which can be used as fuel or for industrial production. Most commonly, biomass refers to plant matter grown for use as biofuel, but it also includes plant or animal matter used for production of fibres, chemicals or heat. Biomass may also include biodegradable wastes that can be burnt as fuel. It excludes organic material which has been transformed by geological processes into substances such as coal or petroleum.
Carbon	Carbon is a chemical element. An abundant nonmetallic, tetravalent element, carbon has several allotropic forms. This element is the basis of the chemistry of all known life.
Carbon dioxide	Carbon dioxide is a chemical compound, normally in a gaseous state, and is composed of one carbon and two oxygen atoms. It is often referred to by its formula CO_2. It is present in the Earth's atmosphere at a concentration of approximately .000383 by volume and is an important greenhouse gas due to its ability to absorb many infrared wavelengths of sunlight, and due to the length of time it stays in the atmosphere.
Residence time	Residence time is a broadly useful concept that expresses how fast something moves through a system in equilibrium. It is the average time a substance spends within a specified region of space, such as a reservoir.
Algae	Algae encompass several groups of relatively simple living aquatic organisms that capture light energy through photosynthesis, using it to convert inorganic substances into organic matter.
Chlorophyll	Chlorophyll is a green pigment found in most plants, algae, and cyanobacteria.
Lake	A lake is a body of water or other liquid of considerable size contained on a body of land. A vast majority are fresh water, and lie in the Northern Hemisphere at higher latitudes. Most have a natural outflow in the form of a river or stream, but some do not, and lose water solely by evaporation and/or underground seepage.
Thermocline	The thermocline is a layer within a body of water or air where the temperature changes rapidly with depth.
Diffusion	Diffusion is the net action of matter, particles or molecules, heat, momentum, or light whose end is to minimize a concentration gradient.
Phytoplankton	Phytoplankton are the autotrophic component of plankton. Most phytoplankton are too small to be individually seen with the unaided eye. However, when present in high enough numbers, they may appear as a green discoloration of the water due to the presence of chlorophyll within their cells.
Equilibrium	Equilibrium is the condition of a system in which competing influences are balanced.

Microorganism	A microorganism is an organism that is microscopic. They can be bacteria, fungi, archaea or protists, but not viruses and prions, which are generally classified as non-living. Micro-organisms are generally single-celled, or unicellular organisms.
Algae	Algae encompass several groups of relatively simple living aquatic organisms that capture light energy through photosynthesis, using it to convert inorganic substances into organic matter.
Phytoplankton	Phytoplankton are the autotrophic component of plankton. Most phytoplankton are too small to be individually seen with the unaided eye. However, when present in high enough numbers, they may appear as a green discoloration of the water due to the presence of chlorophyll within their cells.
Matter	Matter is the substance of which physical objects are composed. Matter can be solid, liquid, plasma or gas. It constitutes the observable universe.
Eutrophication	Eutrophication refers to an increase in the primary productivity of any ecosystem. Eutrophication is caused by the increase of chemical nutrients, typically compounds containing nitrogen or phosphorus. It may occur on land or in water.
Predation	In ecology, predation describes a biological interaction where a predator organism feeds on another living organism or organisms known as prey.[
Attenuation	Attenuation is the reduction in amplitude and intensity of a signal.
Silica	Silica is the oxide of silicon, chemical formula SiO_2, and is known for its hardness as early as the 16th century. It is a principle component in most types of glass and substances such as concrete.
Diatoms	Diatoms are a major group of eukaryotic algae, and are one of the most common types of phytoplankton. Most diatoms are unicellular, although some form chains or simple colonies. A characteristic feature of diatom cells is that they are encased within a unique cell wall made of silica called a frustule.
Competition	Competition between members of a species is the driving force behind evolution and natural selection; especially for resources such as food, water, territory, and sunlight results in the ultimate survival and dominance of the variation of the species best suited for survival.
Chlorophyll	Chlorophyll is a green pigment found in most plants, algae, and cyanobacteria.
Diurnal	A diurnal animal is an animal that is active during the daytime and rests during the night.
Radiation	Radiation as used in physics, is energy in the form of waves or moving subatomic particles.
Plankton	Plankton are any drifting organism that inhabits the water column of oceans, seas, and bodies of fresh water. They are widely considered to be some of the most important organisms on Earth, due to the food supply they provide to most aquatic life.
Extinction	In biology and ecology, extinction is the cessation of existence of a species or group of taxa, reducing biodiversity. The moment of extinction is generally considered to be the death of the last individual of that species.
Detritus	In biology, detritus is non-living particulate organic material. It typically includes the bodies of dead organisms or fragments of organisms or faecal material. Detritus is normally colonised by communities of microorganisms which act to decompose the material.
Primary production	Primary production is the production of organic compounds from atmospheric or aquatic carbon dioxide, principally through the process of photosynthesis, with chemosynthesis being much less important. All life on earth is directly or indirectly reliant on it.
Photosynthesis	Photosynthesis generally, is the synthesis of triose phosphates from sunlight, carbon dioxide

Go to **Cram101.com** for the Practice Tests for this Chapter.

and water.

Lake	A lake is a body of water or other liquid of considerable size contained on a body of land. A vast majority are fresh water, and lie in the Northern Hemisphere at higher latitudes. Most have a natural outflow in the form of a river or stream, but some do not, and lose water solely by evaporation and/or underground seepage.
Carbon	Carbon is a chemical element. An abundant nonmetallic, tetravalent element, carbon has several allotropic forms. This element is the basis of the chemistry of all known life.
Carbon dioxide	Carbon dioxide is a chemical compound, normally in a gaseous state, and is composed of one carbon and two oxygen atoms. It is often referred to by its formula CO_2. It is present in the Earth's atmosphere at a concentration of approximately .000383 by volume and is an important greenhouse gas due to its ability to absorb many infrared wavelengths of sunlight, and due to the length of time it stays in the atmosphere.
Zooplankton	Zooplankton are the heterotrophic component of the plankton that drift in the water column of oceans, seas, and bodies of fresh water. Many zooplankton are too small to be individually seen with the unaided eye.
Carbon cycle	The carbon cycle is the biogeochemical cycle by which carbon is exchanged between the biosphere, geosphere, hydrosphere, and atmosphere of the Earth.
Thermocline	The thermocline is a layer within a body of water or air where the temperature changes rapidly with depth.
Diffusion	Diffusion is the net action of matter, particles or molecules, heat, momentum, or light whose end is to minimize a concentration gradient.
Biomass	Biomass, in the energy production industry, refers to living and recently dead biological material which can be used as fuel or for industrial production. Most commonly, biomass refers to plant matter grown for use as biofuel, but it also includes plant or animal matter used for production of fibres, chemicals or heat. Biomass may also include biodegradable wastes that can be burnt as fuel. It excludes organic material which has been transformed by geological processes into substances such as coal or petroleum.
Pollution	Pollution is the introduction of substances or energy into the environment, resulting in deleterious effects of such a nature as to endanger human health, harm living resources and ecosystems, and impair or interfere with amenities and other legitimate uses of the environment.
Irradiance	Irradiance is radiometry terms for the power of electromagnetic radiation at a surface, per unit area. It is used when the electromagnetic radiation is incident on the surface.
Metabolism	Metabolism is the complete set of chemical reactions that occur in living cells. These processes are the basis of life, allowing cells to grow and reproduce, maintain their structures, and respond to their environments.
Particulates	Particulates are tiny particles of solid or liquid suspended in a gas. They range in size from less than 10 nanometres to more than 100 micrometres in diameter.
Residence time	Residence time is a broadly useful concept that expresses how fast something moves through a system in equilibrium. It is the average time a substance spends within a specified region of space, such as a reservoir.

Phytoplankton	Phytoplankton are the autotrophic component of plankton. Most phytoplankton are too small to be individually seen with the unaided eye. However, when present in high enough numbers, they may appear as a green discoloration of the water due to the presence of chlorophyll within their cells.
Predator	A predator is an organism that feeds on another living organism or organisms known as prey. A predator may or may not kill their prey prior to or during the act of feeding on them.
Plankton	Plankton are any drifting organism that inhabits the water column of oceans, seas, and bodies of fresh water. They are widely considered to be some of the most important organisms on Earth, due to the food supply they provide to most aquatic life.
Zooplankton	Zooplankton are the heterotrophic component of the plankton that drift in the water column of oceans, seas, and bodies of fresh water. Many zooplankton are too small to be individually seen with the unaided eye.
Algae	Algae encompass several groups of relatively simple living aquatic organisms that capture light energy through photosynthesis, using it to convert inorganic substances into organic matter.
Krill	Krill are shrimp-like marine invertebrate animals. These small crustaceans are important organisms of the zooplankton, particularly as food for baleen whales, mantas, whale sharks, crabeater seals and other seals, and a few seabird species that feed almost exclusively on them.
Lake	A lake is a body of water or other liquid of considerable size contained on a body of land. A vast majority are fresh water, and lie in the Northern Hemisphere at higher latitudes. Most have a natural outflow in the form of a river or stream, but some do not, and lose water solely by evaporation and/or underground seepage.
Eutrophication	Eutrophication refers to an increase in the primary productivity of any ecosystem. Eutrophication is caused by the increase of chemical nutrients, typically compounds containing nitrogen or phosphorus. It may occur on land or in water.
Chlorophyll	Chlorophyll is a green pigment found in most plants, algae, and cyanobacteria.
Biomass	Biomass, in the energy production industry, refers to living and recently dead biological material which can be used as fuel or for industrial production. Most commonly, biomass refers to plant matter grown for use as biofuel, but it also includes plant or animal matter used for production of fibres, chemicals or heat. Biomass may also include biodegradable wastes that can be burnt as fuel. It excludes organic material which has been transformed by geological processes into substances such as coal or petroleum.
Detritus	In biology, detritus is non-living particulate organic material. It typically includes the bodies of dead organisms or fragments of organisms or faecal material. Detritus is normally colonised by communities of microorganisms which act to decompose the material.
Predation	In ecology, predation describes a biological interaction where a predator organism feeds on another living organism or organisms known as prey.[
Food web	Food web refers to describe the feeding relationships between species in an ecological community. Typically a food web refers to a graph where only connections are recorded, and a food web or ecosystem network refers to a network where the connections are given weights representing the quantity of nutrients or energy being transferred.
Carnivore	A carnivore is an animal with a diet consisting mainly of meat, whether it comes from animals living or dead. Some animals are considered a carnivore even if their diets contain very little meat but involve preying on other animals. Animals that subsist on a diet consisting only of meat are referred to as an obligate carnivore. Plants that capture and digest insects

Go to **Cram101.com** for the Practice Tests for this Chapter.

are called carnivorous plants. Similarly fungi that capture microscopic animals are often called carnivorous fungi.

Closed system

In thermodynamics, a closed system can exchange heat and work, but not matter, with its surroundings.

Herbivore

An herbivore is an organism that consumes only autotrophs such as plants, algae and photosynthesizing bacteria. By that definition, many fungi, some bacteria, many animals, about 1% of flowering plants and some protists can be considered a herbivore.

Residence time

Residence time is a broadly useful concept that expresses how fast something moves through a system in equilibrium. It is the average time a substance spends within a specified region of space, such as a reservoir.

Go to **Cram101.com** for the Practice Tests for this Chapter.

Lake	A lake is a body of water or other liquid of considerable size contained on a body of land. A vast majority are fresh water, and lie in the Northern Hemisphere at higher latitudes. Most have a natural outflow in the form of a river or stream, but some do not, and lose water solely by evaporation and/or underground seepage.
Eutrophication	Eutrophication refers to an increase in the primary productivity of any ecosystem. Eutrophication is caused by the increase of chemical nutrients, typically compounds containing nitrogen or phosphorus. It may occur on land or in water.
Thermocline	The thermocline is a layer within a body of water or air where the temperature changes rapidly with depth.
Zooplankton	Zooplankton are the heterotrophic component of the plankton that drift in the water column of oceans, seas, and bodies of fresh water. Many zooplankton are too small to be individually seen with the unaided eye.
Algae	Algae encompass several groups of relatively simple living aquatic organisms that capture light energy through photosynthesis, using it to convert inorganic substances into organic matter.
Food web	Food web refers to describe the feeding relationships between species in an ecological community. Typically a food web refers to a graph where only connections are recorded, and a food web or ecosystem network refers to a network where the connections are given weights representing the quantity of nutrients or energy being transferred.
Radiation	Radiation as used in physics, is energy in the form of waves or moving subatomic particles.
Phytoplankton	Phytoplankton are the autotrophic component of plankton. Most phytoplankton are too small to be individually seen with the unaided eye. However, when present in high enough numbers, they may appear as a green discoloration of the water due to the presence of chlorophyll within their cells.
Carnivore	A carnivore is an animal with a diet consisting mainly of meat, whether it comes from animals living or dead. Some animals are considered a carnivore even if their diets contain very little meat but involve preying on other animals. Animals that subsist on a diet consisting only of meat are referred to as an obligate carnivore. Plants that capture and digest insects are called carnivorous plants. Similarly fungi that capture microscopic animals are often called carnivorous fungi.
Chlorophyll	Chlorophyll is a green pigment found in most plants, algae, and cyanobacteria.
Ion	An ion is an atom or group of atoms which have lost or gained one or more electrons, making them negatively or positively charged.
Diffusion	Diffusion is the net action of matter, particles or molecules, heat, momentum, or light whose end is to minimize a concentration gradient.
Extinction	In biology and ecology, extinction is the cessation of existence of a species or group of taxa, reducing biodiversity. The moment of extinction is generally considered to be the death of the last individual of that species.
Herbivore	An herbivore is an organism that consumes only autotrophs such as plants, algae and photosynthesizing bacteria. By that definition, many fungi, some bacteria, many animals, about 1% of flowering plants and some protists can be considered a herbivore.
Carbon	Carbon is a chemical element. An abundant nonmetallic, tetravalent element, carbon has several allotropic forms. This element is the basis of the chemistry of all known life.
Carbon cycle	The carbon cycle is the biogeochemical cycle by which carbon is exchanged between the biosphere, geosphere, hydrosphere, and atmosphere of the Earth.

Matter	Matter is the substance of which physical objects are composed. Matter can be solid, liquid, plasma or gas. It constitutes the observable universe.
Diatoms	Diatoms are a major group of eukaryotic algae, and are one of the most common types of phytoplankton. Most diatoms are unicellular, although some form chains or simple colonies. A characteristic feature of diatom cells is that they are encased within a unique cell wall made of silica called a frustule.
Bacteria	Bacteria are unicellular microorganisms. They are typically a few micrometres long and have many shapes including curved rods, spheres, rods, and spirals.
Sediment	Sediment is any particulate matter that can be transported by fluid flow and which eventually is deposited as a layer of solid particles on the bed or bottom of a body of water or other liquid.
Particulates	Particulates are tiny particles of solid or liquid suspended in a gas. They range in size from less than 10 nanometres to more than 100 micrometres in diameter.

Eutrophication	Eutrophication refers to an increase in the primary productivity of any ecosystem. Eutrophication is caused by the increase of chemical nutrients, typically compounds containing nitrogen or phosphorus. It may occur on land or in water.
Phytoplankton	Phytoplankton are the autotrophic component of plankton. Most phytoplankton are too small to be individually seen with the unaided eye. However, when present in high enough numbers, they may appear as a green discoloration of the water due to the presence of chlorophyll within their cells.
Stream	A stream is a body of water with a current, confined within a bed and banks. Streams are important as conduits in the water cycle, instruments in aquifer recharge, and corridors for fish and wildlife migration.
Lake	A lake is a body of water or other liquid of considerable size contained on a body of land. A vast majority are fresh water, and lie in the Northern Hemisphere at higher latitudes. Most have a natural outflow in the form of a river or stream, but some do not, and lose water solely by evaporation and/or underground seepage.
Nonpoint sources	Nonpoint sources comes from many unidentifiable sources with no specific solution to rectify the proble, making it difficult to regulate. An example would be urban runnoff of items like oil, fertilizers, and lawn chemicals. As rainfall or snowmelt moves over and through the ground, it picks up and carries away natural and human-made pollutants.
Radiation	Radiation as used in physics, is energy in the form of waves or moving subatomic particles.
Evaporation	Evaporation is the process by which molecules in a liquid state become a gas.
Latitude	Latitude gives the location of a place on Earth north or south of the equator. Lines of Latitude are the horizontal lines shown running east-to-west on maps. Technically, Latitude is an angular measurement in degrees ranging from 0° at the Equator to 90° at the poles.
Longitude	Longitude is the east-west geographic coordinate measurement most commonly utilized in cartography and global navigation.
Attenuation	Attenuation is the reduction in amplitude and intensity of a signal.
Island	An island is any piece of land that is completely surrounded by water, above high tide. There are two main types of islands: continental islands and oceanic islands. There are also artificial islands. A grouping of geographically and/or geologically related islands is called an archipelago.
Algae	Algae encompass several groups of relatively simple living aquatic organisms that capture light energy through photosynthesis, using it to convert inorganic substances into organic matter.
Biomass	Biomass, in the energy production industry, refers to living and recently dead biological material which can be used as fuel or for industrial production. Most commonly, biomass refers to plant matter grown for use as biofuel, but it also includes plant or animal matter used for production of fibres, chemicals or heat. Biomass may also include biodegradable wastes that can be burnt as fuel. It excludes organic material which has been transformed by geological processes into substances such as coal or petroleum.
Photosynthesis	Photosynthesis generally, is the synthesis of triose phosphates from sunlight, carbon dioxide and water.
Sediment	Sediment is any particulate matter that can be transported by fluid flow and which eventually is deposited as a layer of solid particles on the bed or bottom of a body of water or other liquid.

Go to **Cram101.com** for the Practice Tests for this Chapter.

Mineral	A mineral is a naturally occurring substance formed through geological processes that has a characteristic chemical composition, a highly ordered atomic structure and specific physical properties. A rock, by comparison, is an aggregate of minerals and need not have a specific chemical composition. Minerals range in composition from pure elements and simple salts to very complex silicates with thousands of known forms.
Phosphorus cycle	The phosphorus cycle is the biogeochemical cycle that describes the movement of phosphorus through the lithosphere, hydrosphere, and biosphere.
Nitrogen	Nitrogen is a chemical element which has the symbol N and atomic number 7. Elemental nitrogen is a colorless, odourless, tasteless and mostly inert diatomic gas at standard conditions, constituting 78.1% by volume of Earth's atmosphere.
Nitrogen cycle	The nitrogen cycle is the biogeochemical cycle that describes the transformations of nitrogen and nitrogen-containing compounds in nature.
Chlorophyll	Chlorophyll is a green pigment found in most plants, algae, and cyanobacteria.
Aquatic	The term aquatic refers to water and can be either a noun or an adjective. Dictionary definitions do not specify what kind of water, although in both general use and in the sciences, the implication is often that of fresh water.
Equilibrium	Equilibrium is the condition of a system in which competing influences are balanced.

Ion	An ion is an atom or group of atoms which have lost or gained one or more electrons, making them negatively or positively charged.
PH scale	The pH scale is a measure of the acidity or alkalinity of a solution. Solutions with less than seven are considered acidic, while those with a number greater than seven are considered basic
Aquatic	The term aquatic refers to water and can be either a noun or an adjective. Dictionary definitions do not specify what kind of water, although in both general use and in the sciences, the implication is often that of fresh water.
Closed system	In thermodynamics, a closed system can exchange heat and work, but not matter, with its surroundings.

Go to **Cram101.com** for the Practice Tests for this Chapter.

Equilibrium	Equilibrium is the condition of a system in which competing influences are balanced.
Residence time	Residence time is a broadly useful concept that expresses how fast something moves through a system in equilibrium. It is the average time a substance spends within a specified region of space, such as a reservoir.
Ion	An ion is an atom or group of atoms which have lost or gained one or more electrons, making them negatively or positively charged.
Lake	A lake is a body of water or other liquid of considerable size contained on a body of land. A vast majority are fresh water, and lie in the Northern Hemisphere at higher latitudes. Most have a natural outflow in the form of a river or stream, but some do not, and lose water solely by evaporation and/or underground seepage.

Go to **Cram101.com** for the Practice Tests for this Chapter.

Ion	An ion is an atom or group of atoms which have lost or gained one or more electrons, making them negatively or positively charged.
Carbon	Carbon is a chemical element. An abundant nonmetallic, tetravalent element, carbon has several allotropic forms. This element is the basis of the chemistry of all known life.
Carbon dioxide	Carbon dioxide is a chemical compound, normally in a gaseous state, and is composed of one carbon and two oxygen atoms. It is often referred to by its formula $CO2$. It is present in the Earth's atmosphere at a concentration of approximately .000383 by volume and is an important greenhouse gas due to its ability to absorb many infrared wavelengths of sunlight, and due to the length of time it stays in the atmosphere.
Equilibrium	Equilibrium is the condition of a system in which competing influences are balanced.
Food web	Food web refers to describe the feeding relationships between species in an ecological community. Typically a food web refers to a graph where only connections are recorded, and a food web or ecosystem network refers to a network where the connections are given weights representing the quantity of nutrients or energy being transferred.
Atmosphere	An atmosphere is a layer of gases that may surround a material body of sufficient mass. The gases are attracted by the gravity of the body, and are retained for a longer duration if gravity is high and the atmosphere's temperature is low. Some planets consist mainly of various gases, and thus have very deep atmospheres.
Precipitation	Precipitation is any product of the condensation of atmospheric water vapor that is deposited on the earth's surface. It occurs when the atmosphere becomes saturated with water vapour and the water condenses and falls out of solution. Air becomes saturated via two processes, cooling and adding moisture.
Fossil	Fossils are the mineralized or otherwise preserved remains or traces of animals, plants, and other organisms. The totality of fossils, both discovered and undiscovered, and their placement in fossiliferous rock formations and sedimentary layers is known as the fossil record.
Lake	A lake is a body of water or other liquid of considerable size contained on a body of land. A vast majority are fresh water, and lie in the Northern Hemisphere at higher latitudes. Most have a natural outflow in the form of a river or stream, but some do not, and lose water solely by evaporation and/or underground seepage.
Photosynthesis	Photosynthesis generally, is the synthesis of triose phosphates from sunlight, carbon dioxide and water.
Island	An island is any piece of land that is completely surrounded by water, above high tide. There are two main types of islands: continental islands and oceanic islands. There are also artificial islands. A grouping of geographically and/or geologically related islands is called an archipelago.

Go to **Cram101.com** for the Practice Tests for this Chapter.

Lake	A lake is a body of water or other liquid of considerable size contained on a body of land. A vast majority are fresh water, and lie in the Northern Hemisphere at higher latitudes. Most have a natural outflow in the form of a river or stream, but some do not, and lose water solely by evaporation and/or underground seepage.
Sediment	Sediment is any particulate matter that can be transported by fluid flow and which eventually is deposited as a layer of solid particles on the bed or bottom of a body of water or other liquid.
Particulates	Particulates are tiny particles of solid or liquid suspended in a gas. They range in size from less than 10 nanometres to more than 100 micrometres in diameter.
Matter	Matter is the substance of which physical objects are composed. Matter can be solid, liquid, plasma or gas. It constitutes the observable universe.
Food web	Food web refers to describe the feeding relationships between species in an ecological community. Typically a food web refers to a graph where only connections are recorded, and a food web or ecosystem network refers to a network where the connections are given weights representing the quantity of nutrients or energy being transferred.
Pollution	Pollution is the introduction of substances or energy into the environment, resulting in deleterious effects of such a nature as to endanger human health, harm living resources and ecosystems, and impair or interfere with amenities and other legitimate uses of the environment.
Bacteria	Bacteria are unicellular microorganisms. They are typically a few micrometres long and have many shapes including curved rods, spheres, rods, and spirals.
Interference	Interference is the addition of two or more waves that results in a new wave pattern. As most commonly used, the term interference usually refers to the interaction of waves which are correlated or coherent with each other, either because they come from the same source or because they have the same or nearly the same frequency.
Aquatic	The term aquatic refers to water and can be either a noun or an adjective. Dictionary definitions do not specify what kind of water, although in both general use and in the sciences, the implication is often that of fresh water.
Eutrophication	Eutrophication refers to an increase in the primary productivity of any ecosystem. Eutrophication is caused by the increase of chemical nutrients, typically compounds containing nitrogen or phosphorus. It may occur on land or in water.
Ecosystem	An ecosystem is a natural unit consisting of all plants, animals and micro organisms in an area functioning together with all the non living physical factors of the environment.
Asbestos	Asbestos describes any of a group of minerals that can be fibrous, many of which are metamorphic and are hydrous magnesium silicates.
Island	An island is any piece of land that is completely surrounded by water, above high tide. There are two main types of islands: continental islands and oceanic islands. There are also artificial islands. A grouping of geographically and/or geologically related islands is called an archipelago.
Atmosphere	An atmosphere is a layer of gases that may surround a material body of sufficient mass. The gases are attracted by the gravity of the body, and are retained for a longer duration if gravity is high and the atmosphere's temperature is low. Some planets consist mainly of various gases, and thus have very deep atmospheres.
Forest	A forest is an area with a high density of trees, historically, a wooded area set aside for hunting. These plant communities cover large areas of the globe and function as animal habitats, hydrologic flow modulators, and soil conservers, constituting one of the most

important aspects of the Earth's biosphere.

Hydrocarbon	In organic chemistry, a hydrocarbon is an organic compound consisting entirely of hydrogen and carbon. With relation to chemical terminology, aromatic hydrocarbons or arenes, alkanes, alkenes and alkyne-based compounds composed entirely of carbon or hydrogen are referred to as "Pure" hydrocarbons, whereas other hydrocarbons with bonded compounds or impurities of sulphur or nitrogen, are referred to as "impure", and remain somewhat erroneously referred to as hydrocarbons.
Polymer	A polymer is a substance composed of molecules with large molecular mass composed of repeating structural units, or monomers, connected by covalent chemical bonds. The term is derived from the Greek words: polys meaning many, and meros meaning parts.
Biomagnification	Biomagnification, also known as bioamplification, or biological magnification is the increase in concentration of a substance, such as the pesticide DDT, that occurs in a food chain as a consequence of: Food chain energetics, low rate of excretion/degradation of the substance.
Toxicity	Toxicity is a measure of the degree to which something is toxic or poisonous. Toxicity can refer to the effect on a whole organism, such as a human or a bacterium or a plant, or to a substructure, such as a cell or an organ.
Invertebrate	Invertebrate is an English word that describes any animal without a spinal column.
Molecule	In chemistry, a molecule is defined as a sufficiently stable electrically neutral group of at least two atoms in a definite arrangement held together by strong chemical bonds.
Air pollution	Air Pollution is a chemical, physical, or biological agent that modifies the natural characteristics of the atmosphere. The atmosphere is a complex, dynamic natural gaseous system that is essential to support life on planet Earth. Stratospheric ozone depletion due to air pollution has long been recognized as a threat to human health as well as to the Earth's ecosystems. Worldwide air pollution is responsible for large numbers of deaths and cases of respiratory disease.
Bioaccumulation	Bioaccumulation occurs when an organism absorbs a toxic substance at a rate greater than that at which the substance is lost.
Fossil	Fossils are the mineralized or otherwise preserved remains or traces of animals, plants, and other organisms. The totality of fossils, both discovered and undiscovered, and their placement in fossiliferous rock formations and sedimentary layers is known as the fossil record.
Herbicide	A herbicide is a pesticide used to kill unwanted plants. They kill specific targets while leaving the desired crop relatively unharmed.
Porosity	Porosity is a measure of the void spaces in a material, and is measured as a fraction, between 0–1, or as a percentage between 0–100%.
Clay	Clay is a term used to describe a group of hydrous aluminium phyllosilicate minerals, that are typically less than 2 micrometres in diameter. Clay consists of a variety of phyllosilicate minerals rich in silicon and aluminium oxides and hydroxides which include variable amounts of structural water. Clays are generally formed by the chemical weathering of silicate-bearing rocks by carbonic acid but some are formed by hydrothermal activity.
Diffusion	Diffusion is the net action of matter, particles or molecules, heat, momentum, or light whose end is to minimize a concentration gradient.
Attenuation	Attenuation is the reduction in amplitude and intensity of a signal.
Residence time	Residence time is a broadly useful concept that expresses how fast something moves through a system in equilibrium. It is the average time a substance spends within a specified region of

Go to **Cram101.com** for the Practice Tests for this Chapter.

space, such as a reservoir.

Matter	Matter is the substance of which physical objects are composed. Matter can be solid, liquid, plasma or gas. It constitutes the observable universe.
Ion	An ion is an atom or group of atoms which have lost or gained one or more electrons, making them negatively or positively charged.
Equilibrium	Equilibrium is the condition of a system in which competing influences are balanced.
Sediment	Sediment is any particulate matter that can be transported by fluid flow and which eventually is deposited as a layer of solid particles on the bed or bottom of a body of water or other liquid.
Porosity	Porosity is a measure of the void spaces in a material, and is measured as a fraction, between 0–1, or as a percentage between 0–100%.
Fog	Fog is a cloud in contact with the ground. It differs from other clouds only in that fog touches the surface of the Earth.
Phytoplankton	Phytoplankton are the autotrophic component of plankton. Most phytoplankton are too small to be individually seen with the unaided eye. However, when present in high enough numbers, they may appear as a green discoloration of the water due to the presence of chlorophyll within their cells.
Drainage	Drainage is the natural or artificial removal of surface and sub-surface water from a given area. Many agricultural soils need drainage to improve production or to manage water supplies.
Drainage basin	A drainage basin is a region of land where water from rain or snow melt drains downhill into a body of water, such as a river, lake, dam, estuary, wetland, sea or ocean. The drainage basin includes both the streams and rivers that convey the water as well as the land surfaces from which water drains into those channels. The drainage basin acts like a funnel - collecting all the water within the area covered by the basin and channeling it into a waterway.
Photosynthesis	Photosynthesis generally, is the synthesis of triose phosphates from sunlight, carbon dioxide and water.
Diffusion	Diffusion is the net action of matter, particles or molecules, heat, momentum, or light whose end is to minimize a concentration gradient.
Atmosphere	An atmosphere is a layer of gases that may surround a material body of sufficient mass. The gases are attracted by the gravity of the body, and are retained for a longer duration if gravity is high and the atmosphere's temperature is low. Some planets consist mainly of various gases, and thus have very deep atmospheres.
Lake	A lake is a body of water or other liquid of considerable size contained on a body of land. A vast majority are fresh water, and lie in the Northern Hemisphere at higher latitudes. Most have a natural outflow in the form of a river or stream, but some do not, and lose water solely by evaporation and/or underground seepage.
Island	An island is any piece of land that is completely surrounded by water, above high tide. There are two main types of islands: continental islands and oceanic islands. There are also artificial islands. A grouping of geographically and/or geologically related islands is called an archipelago.
Pesticide	The U.S Environmental Protection Agency defines a pesticide as "any substance or mixture of substances intended for preventing, destroying, repelling, or lessening the damage of any pest".
Water vapor	Water vapor is the gas phase of water. Water vapor is one state of the water cycle within the

	hydrosphere. Water vapor can be produced from the evaporation of liquid water or from the sublimation of ice. Under normal atmospheric conditions, water vapor is continuously evaporating and condensing.
Vapor	Vapor is the gas phase component of a another state of matter which does not completely fill its container. It is distinguished from the pure gas phase by the presence of the same substance in another state of matter. Hence when a liquid has completely evaporated, it is said that the system has been completely transformed to the gas phase.
Eutrophication	Eutrophication refers to an increase in the primary productivity of any ecosystem. Eutrophication is caused by the increase of chemical nutrients, typically compounds containing nitrogen or phosphorus. It may occur on land or in water.
Recycling	Recycling is the reprocessing of materials into new products. It prevents useful material resources being wasted, reduces the consumption of raw materials and reduces energy usage, and hence greenhouse gas emissions, compared to virgin production.
Eutrophic lake	A eutrophic lake is a lake with high primary productivity, the result of high nutrient content. These lakes are subject to excessive algal blooms, resulting in murky water and poor water quality. The bottom waters of such lakes are commonly deficient in oxygen.
Particulates	Particulates are tiny particles of solid or liquid suspended in a gas. They range in size from less than 10 nanometres to more than 100 micrometres in diameter.
Toxicity	Toxicity is a measure of the degree to which something is toxic or poisonous. Toxicity can refer to the effect on a whole organism, such as a human or a bacterium or a plant, or to a substructure, such as a cell or an organ.
Ecosystem	An ecosystem is a natural unit consisting of all plants, animals and micro organisms in an area functioning together with all the non living physical factors of the environment.

Particulates	Particulates are tiny particles of solid or liquid suspended in a gas. They range in size from less than 10 nanometres to more than 100 micrometres in diameter.
Matter	Matter is the substance of which physical objects are composed. Matter can be solid, liquid, plasma or gas. It constitutes the observable universe.
Atmosphere	An atmosphere is a layer of gases that may surround a material body of sufficient mass. The gases are attracted by the gravity of the body, and are retained for a longer duration if gravity is high and the atmosphere's temperature is low. Some planets consist mainly of various gases, and thus have very deep atmospheres.
Radiation	Radiation as used in physics, is energy in the form of waves or moving subatomic particles.
Attenuation	Attenuation is the reduction in amplitude and intensity of a signal.
Weather	The weather is the set of all extant phenomena in a given atmosphere at a given time. The term usually refers to the activity of these phenomena over short periods, as opposed to the term climate, which refers to the average atmospheric conditions over longer periods of time.
Lake	A lake is a body of water or other liquid of considerable size contained on a body of land. A vast majority are fresh water, and lie in the Northern Hemisphere at higher latitudes. Most have a natural outflow in the form of a river or stream, but some do not, and lose water solely by evaporation and/or underground seepage.
Wavelength	In physics, wavelength is the distance between repeating units of a propagating wave of a given frequency. It is commonly designated by the Greek letter lambda. Examples of wave-like phenonomena are light, water waves, and sound waves. Wavelength of a sine wave.In a wave, a property varies with the position.
Bacteria	Bacteria are unicellular microorganisms. They are typically a few micrometres long and have many shapes including curved rods, spheres, rods, and spirals.
Wave	A wave is a disturbance that propagates through space or spacetime, transferring energy and momentum and sometimes angular momentum.
Frequency	Frequency is the measurement of the number of occurrences of a repeated event per unit of time. It is also defined as the rate of change of phase of a sinusoidal waveform.
Solar power	Solar power is Solar Radiation emitted from our sun. It has been used in many traditional technologies for centuries, and has come into widespread use where other power supplies are absent, such as in remote locations and in space.
Ultraviolet	Ultraviolet light is electromagnetic radiation with a wavelength shorter than that of visible light, but longer than soft X-rays. The color violet has the shortest wavelength in the visible spectrum. UV light has a shorter wavelength than that of violet light.
Altitude	Altitude is the elevation of an object from a known level or datum. Common datums are mean sea level and the surface of the World Geodetic System geoid, used by Global Positioning System. In aviation, altitude is measured in feet. For non-aviation uses, altitude may be measured in other units such as metres or miles.
Latitude	Latitude gives the location of a place on Earth north or south of the equator. Lines of Latitude are the horizontal lines shown running east-to-west on maps. Technically, Latitude is an angular measurement in degrees ranging from 0° at the Equator to 90° at the poles.
Diurnal	A diurnal animal is an animal that is active during the daytime and rests during the night.
Extinction	In biology and ecology, extinction is the cessation of existence of a species or group of taxa, reducing biodiversity. The moment of extinction is generally considered to be the death of the last individual of that species.

Irradiance	Irradiance is radiometry terms for the power of electromagnetic radiation at a surface, per unit area. It is used when the electromagnetic radiation is incident on the surface.
Molecule	In chemistry, a molecule is defined as a sufficiently stable electrically neutral group of at least two atoms in a definite arrangement held together by strong chemical bonds.
Electron	The electron is a fundamental subatomic particle that carries a negative electric charge.
Anion	An anion is a negetive ion.
Chlorophyll	Chlorophyll is a green pigment found in most plants, algae, and cyanobacteria.
Oligotrophic	Oligotrophic refers to any environment that offers little to sustain life. This term is usually used to describe bodies of water or soils with very low nutrient levels.
Eutrophic lake	A eutrophic lake is a lake with high primary productivity, the result of high nutrient content. These lakes are subject to excessive algal blooms, resulting in murky water and poor water quality. The bottom waters of such lakes are commonly deficient in oxygen.
Turbidity	Turbidity is a cloudiness or haziness of water caused by individual particles that are generally invisible to the naked eye, thus being much like smoke in air. Turbidity is generally caused by phytoplankton. Measurement of turbidity is a key test of water quality.
Microorganism	A microorganism is an organism that is microscopic. They can be bacteria, fungi, archaea or protists, but not viruses and prions, which are generally classified as non-living. Micro-organisms are generally single-celled, or unicellular organisms.
Organic compound	An organic compound is any member of a large class of chemical compounds whose molecules contain carbon.
Organism	In biology and ecology, an organism is a living complex adaptive system of organs that influence each other in such a way that they function in some way as a stable whole.
Metabolism	Metabolism is the complete set of chemical reactions that occur in living cells. These processes are the basis of life, allowing cells to grow and reproduce, maintain their structures, and respond to their environments.
Toxicity	Toxicity is a measure of the degree to which something is toxic or poisonous. Toxicity can refer to the effect on a whole organism, such as a human or a bacterium or a plant, or to a substructure, such as a cell or an organ.
Biomass	Biomass, in the energy production industry, refers to living and recently dead biological material which can be used as fuel or for industrial production. Most commonly, biomass refers to plant matter grown for use as biofuel, but it also includes plant or animal matter used for production of fibres, chemicals or heat. Biomass may also include biodegradable wastes that can be burnt as fuel. It excludes organic material which has been transformed by geological processes into substances such as coal or petroleum.
Oligotrophic lake	An oligotrophic lake is a lake with low primary productivity, the result of low nutrient content. These lakes have low algal production, and consequently, often have very clear waters, with high drinking-water quality.
Stream	A stream is a body of water with a current, confined within a bed and banks. Streams are important as conduits in the water cycle, instruments in aquifer recharge, and corridors for fish and wildlife migration.
Aquatic	The term aquatic refers to water and can be either a noun or an adjective. Dictionary definitions do not specify what kind of water, although in both general use and in the sciences, the implication is often that of fresh water.
Pesticide	The U.S Environmental Protection Agency defines a pesticide as "any substance or mixture of

substances intended for preventing, destroying, repelling, or lessening the damage of any pest".

Equilibrium

Equilibrium is the condition of a system in which competing influences are balanced.

Oxide

An oxide is a chemical compound containing an oxygen atom and other elements. Most of the earth's crust consists of them. They result when elements are oxidized by air.

Ozone

Ozone is a triatomic molecule, consisting of three oxygen atoms. It is an allotrope of oxygen that is much less stable than the diatomic species O_2. Ground-level ozone is an air pollutant with harmful effects on the respiratory systems of animals. On the other hand, ozone in the upper atmosphere protects living organisms by preventing damaging ultraviolet light from reaching the Earth's surface.

Ion

An ion is an atom or group of atoms which have lost or gained one or more electrons, making them negatively or positively charged.

Sediment

Sediment is any particulate matter that can be transported by fluid flow and which eventually is deposited as a layer of solid particles on the bed or bottom of a body of water or other liquid.

Go to **Cram101.com** for the Practice Tests for this Chapter.

Nuclear energy	Nuclear energy is energy released from the atomic nucleus.
Particulates	Particulates are tiny particles of solid or liquid suspended in a gas. They range in size from less than 10 nanometres to more than 100 micrometres in diameter.
Matter	Matter is the substance of which physical objects are composed. Matter can be solid, liquid, plasma or gas. It constitutes the observable universe.
Radioactive decay	Radioactive decay is the process in which an unstable atomic nucleus loses energy by emitting radiation in the form of particles or electromagnetic waves.
Atoms	Atoms are the fundamental building blocks of chemistry, and are conserved in chemical reactions.
Lake	A lake is a body of water or other liquid of considerable size contained on a body of land. A vast majority are fresh water, and lie in the Northern Hemisphere at higher latitudes. Most have a natural outflow in the form of a river or stream, but some do not, and lose water solely by evaporation and/or underground seepage.
Diffusion	Diffusion is the net action of matter, particles or molecules, heat, momentum, or light whose end is to minimize a concentration gradient.
Porosity	Porosity is a measure of the void spaces in a material, and is measured as a fraction, between 0–1, or as a percentage between 0–100%.
Island	An island is any piece of land that is completely surrounded by water, above high tide. There are two main types of islands: continental islands and oceanic islands. There are also artificial islands. A grouping of geographically and/or geologically related islands is called an archipelago.
Ion	An ion is an atom or group of atoms which have lost or gained one or more electrons, making them negatively or positively charged.
Speciation	Speciation is the evolutionary process by which new biological species arise.
Toxicity	Toxicity is a measure of the degree to which something is toxic or poisonous. Toxicity can refer to the effect on a whole organism, such as a human or a bacterium or a plant, or to a substructure, such as a cell or an organ.
Equilibrium	Equilibrium is the condition of a system in which competing influences are balanced.
Recycling	Recycling is the reprocessing of materials into new products. It prevents useful material resources being wasted, reduces the consumption of raw materials and reduces energy usage, and hence greenhouse gas emissions, compared to virgin production.
Stream	A stream is a body of water with a current, confined within a bed and banks. Streams are important as conduits in the water cycle, instruments in aquifer recharge, and corridors for fish and wildlife migration.
Precipitation	Precipitation is any product of the condensation of atmospheric water vapor that is deposited on the earth's surface. It occurs when the atmosphere becomes saturated with water vapour and the water condenses and falls out of solution. Air becomes saturated via two processes, cooling and adding moisture.
Benthos	Benthos are the organisms which live on, in, or near the seabed. Although the term derived from the Greek for "depths of the sea", the term is also used in freshwater biology to refer to organisms at the bottoms of freshwater bodies of water, such as lakes, rivers, and streams.
Competition	Competition between members of a species is the driving force behind evolution and natural selection; especially for resources such as food, water, territory, and sunlight results in

the ultimate survival and dominance of the variation of the species best suited for survival.

Lake	A lake is a body of water or other liquid of considerable size contained on a body of land. A vast majority are fresh water, and lie in the Northern Hemisphere at higher latitudes. Most have a natural outflow in the form of a river or stream, but some do not, and lose water solely by evaporation and/or underground seepage.
Stream	A stream is a body of water with a current, confined within a bed and banks. Streams are important as conduits in the water cycle, instruments in aquifer recharge, and corridors for fish and wildlife migration.
Sediment	Sediment is any particulate matter that can be transported by fluid flow and which eventually is deposited as a layer of solid particles on the bed or bottom of a body of water or other liquid.
Island	An island is any piece of land that is completely surrounded by water, above high tide. There are two main types of islands: continental islands and oceanic islands. There are also artificial islands. A grouping of geographically and/or geologically related islands is called an archipelago.
Matter	Matter is the substance of which physical objects are composed. Matter can be solid, liquid, plasma or gas. It constitutes the observable universe.
Diffusion	Diffusion is the net action of matter, particles or molecules, heat, momentum, or light whose end is to minimize a concentration gradient.
Nonpoint sources	Nonpoint sources comes from many unidentifiable sources with no specific solution to rectify the proble, making it difficult to regulate. An example would be urban runoff of items like oil, fertilizers, and lawn chemicals. As rainfall or snowmelt moves over and through the ground, it picks up and carries away natural and human-made pollutants.
Groundwater	Groundwater is water located beneath the ground surface in soil pore spaces and in the fractures of geologic formations. Groundwater is recharged from, and eventually flows to, the surface naturally; natural discharge often occurs at springs and seeps, streams and can often form oases or wetlands.
Eutrophication	Eutrophication refers to an increase in the primary productivity of any ecosystem. Eutrophication is caused by the increase of chemical nutrients, typically compounds containing nitrogen or phosphorus. It may occur on land or in water.
Fog	Fog is a cloud in contact with the ground. It differs from other clouds only in that fog touches the surface of the Earth.
Porosity	Porosity is a measure of the void spaces in a material, and is measured as a fraction, between 0–1, or as a percentage between 0–100%.

Lake	A lake is a body of water or other liquid of considerable size contained on a body of land. A vast majority are fresh water, and lie in the Northern Hemisphere at higher latitudes. Most have a natural outflow in the form of a river or stream, but some do not, and lose water solely by evaporation and/or underground seepage.
Ecosystem	An ecosystem is a natural unit consisting of all plants, animals and micro organisms in an area functioning together with all the non living physical factors of the environment.
Aquatic	The term aquatic refers to water and can be either a noun or an adjective. Dictionary definitions do not specify what kind of water, although in both general use and in the sciences, the implication is often that of fresh water.
Organism	In biology and ecology, an organism is a living complex adaptive system of organs that influence each other in such a way that they function in some way as a stable whole.
Bioaccumulation	Bioaccumulation occurs when an organism absorbs a toxic substance at a rate greater than that at which the substance is lost.
Biomagnification	Biomagnification, also known as bioamplification, or biological magnification is the increase in concentration of a substance, such as the pesticide DDT, that occurs in a food chain as a consequence of: Food chain energetics, low rate of excretion/degradation of the substance.
Food web	Food web refers to describe the feeding relationships between species in an ecological community. Typically a food web refers to a graph where only connections are recorded, and a food web or ecosystem network refers to a network where the connections are given weights representing the quantity of nutrients or energy being transferred.
Metabolism	Metabolism is the complete set of chemical reactions that occur in living cells. These processes are the basis of life, allowing cells to grow and reproduce, maintain their structures, and respond to their environments.
Biomass	Biomass, in the energy production industry, refers to living and recently dead biological material which can be used as fuel or for industrial production. Most commonly, biomass refers to plant matter grown for use as biofuel, but it also includes plant or animal matter used for production of fibres, chemicals or heat. Biomass may also include biodegradable wastes that can be burnt as fuel. It excludes organic material which has been transformed by geological processes into substances such as coal or petroleum.
Zooplankton	Zooplankton are the heterotrophic component of the plankton that drift in the water column of oceans, seas, and bodies of fresh water. Many zooplankton are too small to be individually seen with the unaided eye.
Phytoplankton	Phytoplankton are the autotrophic component of plankton. Most phytoplankton are too small to be individually seen with the unaided eye. However, when present in high enough numbers, they may appear as a green discoloration of the water due to the presence of chlorophyll within their cells.
Shoreline	A shoreline is the fringe of land at the edge of a large body of water, such as an ocean, sea, or lake. A strict definition is the strip of land along a water body that is alternately exposed and covered by waves and tides.
Predator	A predator is an organism that feeds on another living organism or organisms known as prey. A predator may or may not kill their prey prior to or during the act of feeding on them.
Plankton	Plankton are any drifting organism that inhabits the water column of oceans, seas, and bodies of fresh water. They are widely considered to be some of the most important organisms on Earth, due to the food supply they provide to most aquatic life.
Gill	A gill is a respiration organ that functions for the extraction of oxygen from water and the excretion of carbon dioxide. They are usually thin plates of tissue, branches, or slender

Go to **Cram101.com** for the Practice Tests for this Chapter.

tufted processes and, with the exception of some aquatic insects, they contain blood or coelomic fluid, which exchanges gases through their thin walls.

Detritus	In biology, detritus is non-living particulate organic material. It typically includes the bodies of dead organisms or fragments of organisms or faecal material. Detritus is normally colonised by communities of microorganisms which act to decompose the material.
Sediment	Sediment is any particulate matter that can be transported by fluid flow and which eventually is deposited as a layer of solid particles on the bed or bottom of a body of water or other liquid.
Diffusion	Diffusion is the net action of matter, particles or molecules, heat, momentum, or light whose end is to minimize a concentration gradient.
Predation	In ecology, predation describes a biological interaction where a predator organism feeds on another living organism or organisms known as prey.[
Benthos	Benthos are the organisms which live on, in, or near the seabed. Although the term derived from the Greek for "depths of the sea", the term is also used in freshwater biology to refer to organisms at the bottoms of freshwater bodies of water, such as lakes, rivers, and streams.
Invertebrate	Invertebrate is an English word that describes any animal without a spinal column.